DARE TO DREAM AGAIN

Embrace Your Worth
Transform Your Life
Achieve Your Dreams

Rosalinda Rivera

Copyright ©2024 by Rosalinda Rivera

Scripture quotations marked (NLT) are taken from the Holy Bible, New Living Translation, copyright ©1996, 2004, 2015 by Tyndale House Foundation. Used by permission of Tyndale House Publishers, a Division of Tyndale House Ministries, Carol Stream, Illinois 60188. All rights reserved. Scripture taken from the New King James Version®. Copyright © 1982 by Thomas Nelson. Used by permission. All rights reserved. Scripture quotations taken from The Holy Bible, New International Version®, NIV® Copyright © 1973, 1978, 1984, 2011 by Biblica, Inc.™ Used by permission. All rights reserved worldwide. "Scripture quotations are from The ESV® Bible (The Holy Bible, English Standard Version®), copy-right © 2001 by Crossway, a publishing ministry of Good News Publishers. Used by permission. All rights reserved." Scripture marked NASB are from the NEW AMERICAN STANDARD BIBLE®, Copyright ©1960,1962, 1963,1968,1971,1972,1973,1975,1977,1995 by The Lockman Foundation. Used by per-mission. Scripture quotations marked NLV are taken from the New Life Version, copyright © 1969 and 2003. Used by permission of Barbour Publishing, Inc., Uhrichsville, Ohio 44683. All rights reserved.

Dare to Dream Again
Embrace Your Worth   Transform Your Life
Achieve Your Dreams

Rosalinda Rivera
https://rosalinda.live

ISBN# 979-8-218-40747-6
First Edition

LionLab

11533 Busy Street, Suite 107
N. Chesterfield, VA 23236
www.lionlab.net
www.lionlab.promos.com

No part of this book may be reproduced or transmitted in any form or by any means, electronic or mechanical – including photocopying, recording, or by any information storage and retrieval system – without permission in writing from the publisher except in the case of brief quotations embodied in critical articles or reviews.

1   2   3   4   5   28   27   26   25   24

"Hey. Don't ever let somebody tell you... You can't do something. Not even me. All right?

You got a dream... You gotta protect it. People can't do somethin' themselves, they wanna tell you you can't do it. If you want somethin', go get it. Period."

— Christopher Gardner
The Pursuit of Happyness

Contents

Introduction: Dream Big 9

Week 1: Embracing Your Dreams:
It's Not Too Late to Have an Adventure 13

Week 2: Discover Your Purpose:
Unveil Your True Calling 23

Week 3: Defy Limiting Beliefs:
Break Barriers and Embrace Potential 37

Week 4: Develop Resilience:
Transforming Setbacks Into Opportunities 47

Week 5: Embrace Fearlessness:
Conquer Doubt and Choose Courage 63

Week 6: Reach Beyond the Sky:
Developing Infinite Potential 75

Week 7: Implementation:
Turning Dreams Into Reality 93

Appendix: Passions and Proficiency Worksheet 110
Bonus *7 Game-Changing Habits* Planners 112

Endnotes 121
About the Author 122

My prayer for you...

Dear Heavenly Father,

As I embark on this journey with my readers, I come before You with a heart full of gratitude and anticipation. Thank You for the opportunity to inspire and encourage others to pursue their dreams with courage and determination.

Lord, I pray for each reader who picks up this book, that they may feel Your presence guiding them every step of the way. Give them the courage to dare to dream again, to believe in the unique gifts and talents You have placed within them, and to trust in Your perfect plan for their lives.

May Your light shine brightly through the pages of this book, illuminating the path to their dreams and igniting a fire within their souls to pursue them relentlessly. Help them overcome obstacles, persevere in the face of adversity, and never lose sight of the dreams You have planted in their hearts.

In Jesus' Name

Amen.

Introduction

Dream Big!

Embarking on a new journey is a large-part exhilarating, a robust slice of exhaustion, with a dollop of quietly bracing for abject humiliation. Stepping into the unknown is daunting, so God gives us the courage to move when we're shaking at the knees. Because we cannot reach a dream that we're unwilling to acknowledge, I will say it to you again: I am praying for you, and I'm proud of you for admitting you want more; whatever God has — all of it!

What dreams have you stashed away, thinking they're too late or too crazy to come true?

When your soul knows it's time, but memories of past attempts try to convince you that you're not ready, one of them is lying.

If you're reading this book, it's because deep down, there's a glimmer of hope that maybe, just maybe, you still believe in going back to school, starting a business, writing that book, shifting careers, or finding your person.

Perhaps you have tried things in the past that haven't worked out, maybe you're living your best life now, or maybe you're skeptical because your dreams seem to have crashed and failed or cost you something you were not prepared to pay. Whatever your current situation or mindset, purchasing this book is a bold first step to declaring and admitting that you're ready to let go of your fears and pursue your dreams. When your soul knows it's time, but memories of past attempts try to convince you that you're not ready, one of them is lying.

> "Forget the former things; do not dwell on the past. See, I am doing a new thing! Now it springs up; do you not perceive it? I am making a way in the wilderness and streams in the wasteland."
>
> — Isaiah 43:18-19 (NIV)

Position. Prepare. Push. Prevail!

Today is about daring to begin to dream again. It's about counting the losses and putting them behind you just as the sun rises, leaving the night behind and ushering in a new day. In this new day, you will wake with a store of energy, a fresh vision, renewed commitment, and determination. You will be greeted with God's mercies anew — every morning from now until you're standing inside your painting, living within the blessings and objectives of God's design for you.

> **Recall any setback that might cause you to hesitate and redefine it to motivate.**

This is your day to **Dare to Dream Again.**

Your partner in dream-chasing,

Rosalinda

I have a simple system that will help you make serious progress towards your goals. Get ready for your Weekly Dream Sessions – it's time to turn those dreams into reality!

Let's start with a few basic practices to carry through each session:

1. **Schedule** your Dream Sessions. Pick a day and time that works best for you — maybe Sunday evenings for some chill reflection or Saturday mornings to kickstart your day with dream-building vibes.

2. **Reflect** on the past week. Take a look back and celebrate those wins, big or small, and acknowledge any challenges or setbacks. It's all part of the journey!

3. **Set Goals** for the week ahead. What steps do you need to take to get closer to your dreams? Write them down, get specific, and let's make it happen!

4. **Outline Tasks** by breaking goals into smaller steps to tackle throughout the week. Assign deadlines, stay focused, and keep that momentum going!

5. **Block Time** dedicated to working on each assignment. Treat these blocks like VIP appointments with yourself — no distractions allowed! Do not reschedule or cancel on your dreams.

6. **Stay Flexible**, adaptable, and open-minded, willing to adjust your plans and accept wise counsel. Life can throw some wild four-seam fastballs, but you've got this!

7. **Review and Prepare** for the coming week. Recall any setback that might cause you to hesitate and redefine it to motivate. Adjust your thinking, give yourself a pep talk, and focus your goal at the forefront of your mind. Move forward.

With our Weekly Dream Sessions in place, we're ready to crush those goals and make some serious magic happen. God is doing a significant thing in your life. You sense it; I know you do. **Let's do this!**

Your prayer of committment...

> Lord, I commit my hopes and dreams into Your hands, knowing that You are the ultimate Dream Giver and the author of all our stories. May Your will be done in my life. Help me dare to dream again, and I will trust You with the details. I will put no limits on my dreams because You are a God who does amazing things beyond my understanding. I don't want to go one more year without seeing my dreams coming true. I give You all the praise and all the glory in the good times and the difficult moments. I'm counting on open doors, great connections, and Godly friendships, networks and support.
>
> In Jesus' name, I pray.
>
> Amen.

WEEK 1

Embracing Your Dreams
It's Not Too Late to Have an Adventure

Have you ever been the one to blow out the flame on your ideas? You know, there was a time when I found myself in a similar spot. I had poured so much of myself into helping others achieve their goals that I was exhausted. Sitting at my vanity set, looking into the mirror, I thought it was past time for a serious heart-to-heart.

"Rosalinda, you've done so much good. You've helped your kids, your parents, people in ministry and non-profits. But maybe it's too late for your dreams."

I even called my husband over to listen to my song of regret and disappointment. Carlos is naturally an encourager, but I was fully committed to my pity party by this point, and going under quickly.

As I sank into discouraged lethargy, it hit me like a sledgehammer of lightning. I realized that I had let the flame of my dreams burn out. Totally gone. Not even a spit of spark. And you know what? I started convincing myself that maybe it was too late to reignite it. The fire was doused by a tsunami of "lost" time, and I felt that all my matches were tear-soaked and useless. Sure, there were some pretty sweet opportunities in days past, but that was then. The *now* felt empty, and the future didn't appear to be preparing itself for me or my desires.

Why bother trying again when someone else's needs can suddenly swoop in and steal the show? Could this be another set-up for a letdown?

Those thoughts could have been where it ended, but deeper down was this little voice (we'll call her my inner cheerleader):

Hey, you've got big dreams! Don't let 'em go to waste!

At some point, I'll tell you about my "impressive" cheer squad days. For now, I'll admit that an internal supporter with a megaphone got me thinking.

Maybe I wasn't as content with the status quo as I thought. Maybe, just maybe, there was more to life than *Netflix* marathons and takeout dinners. As the warmth of hope and faith increased, the weariness of doubt started to dry up, and I started searching for what I needed to build a fire.

Reigniting the Flame Within

It is never too late to chase — and catch — your dreams! No matter how crazy or far-fetched they might seem in your personal life stage or situation, embrace the permanence of your purpose. I just recently flipped over to the *50 and Over Club*. Guess what? I'm proud to say I'm still kicking, vibrant, and full of ideas. You are never too young or old to go after your God-given purpose.

So here we are, my friend. — Week One. It's time to dust off those dreams, grab 'em by the horns, and give 'em a good shake! We will confront the doubts and fears head-on because, let's face it — they've overstayed their welcome.

Together, let's have a good laugh at our own expense. Why take life so seriously, right? We'll start chipping away at those pesky limiting beliefs that have been holding us back.

"I'm not good enough."

"I don't deserve success."

"I can't change my future."

"It's too late for me."

"I've made too many mistakes."

Will you be unguarded enough to identify controlling thoughts and confining behaviors? Are you undaunted in your commitment to challenge and change them?

Grab a cup of coffee or tea, or whatever works for ya' and let's get this party started! You, my friend, are destined for greatness. I can't wait to see you shine!

To Dream the Impossible Dream

What is your dream? What drives you to wake up each morning with passion and push through late hours until you accomplish it?

Have you ever stopped to ponder what truly sets your soul on fire? What makes your heart beat a little faster, and your spirit soar? That indescribable feeling of purpose is the driving force behind it all. While our aspirations change, sometimes drastically, over time, they are as individual as our tongue-prints (yes, you read that correctly).

Throughout my life, I have wanted to be a ballerina, a firefighter, and the President of the United States. I didn't quite accomplish my goals precisely the way I intended. Still, I choreographed a choir of 100 youths for fifteen years. I rooted for the firefighters who came to extinguish the fire I started in my college dorm when bagels got stuck in the toaster. I am the CEO and President of five separate entities. Also, I did a brief stint as a paleontologist when I was twelve after a visit to the Smithsonian. My great find of dinosaur bones in the field behind the barn turned out to be a cow carcass — a career low for any archaeologist.

Those examples of *What do I want to be when I grow up* were fun, but I don't want you to miss this powerful point: God plants desires in us and sews them like a thread through the tapestry of our years. I can see some of those childhood interests coming through even now. I am not digging up bones, but God has trained me to be a locater and excavator of what lies beneath, layered below the surface of a person. Now, I mentor people through the process of digging deep to find the source of their behaviors and brokenness to map out a healthy future. Every day, I wake up with a passion to inspire, uplift, and empower those around me. That joy of helping others and positively impacting their lives lights a fire under me. It fuels my spirit and ignites my drive to keep pushing forward, even when the road gets tough. What is your great motivator?

What idea or activity wakes you up in the morning with excitement bubbling in your veins? What sets your soul on fire, fills you with an unquenchable thirst for success, and keeps you burning the midnight oil until you make your dreams a reality? Take a moment to reflect on your strongest desires and aspirations. No dream is too big, too wild, or too costly — financially, physically, or emotionally.

Whether pursuing a creative passion, making a difference in your community, climbing Everest, skiing the Alps of Zermatt, Switzerland, or achieving personal growth and fulfillment, your dream is waiting to be uncovered. How much longer will you make it wait? I encourage you to take that first step today.

Following your purpose is a journey of self-discovery and exploration. Set aside some time for introspection, journaling, or simply quiet contemplation. Ask yourself what brings you joy, fulfillment, and a sense of purpose. Ask the Lord to help you tune in to your innermost desires, listen to your heart's whispers, and embrace the unique gifts and talents that make you who you are.

If you have read any of my books, you will know I'm a coach. You will hear that voice as you continue this journey with me in the coming weeks. I will encourage you, but have no doubt: I will push you to go farther than you thought you could.

Do you know who holds the most Olympic gold medals in the world? If you are like most people, you will answer Michael Phelps, and you are right. Do you know who his coach is?

Bob Bowman started coaching Michael when the swimmer was only eleven and has coached him throughout his career.[1] Phelps would have never gotten to where he did without Coach Bob, but I am sure there were times he wanted to hide that whistle. Michael may have even had a few choice words for his coach when Bowman made him swim an extra 500 meters. But those extra laps, drills, added practices, and sacrificial lifestyle are why Michael Phelps is the record holder with twenty-eight Olympic medals.

A great coach is a creative leader with a clear vision to inspire and equip, and dedicated to the personal growth of the *players* as they pursue the win. Through these pages and many hours of prayer, I have committed to your development. I want you to win.

Success does not come easy, but isn't your dream worth pursuing with every ounce of passion and determination you possess? I believe it is, so let's get moving on this journey of discovery and unlock the endless possibilities that await us.

Plot Twist: The Unexpected Way Dreams Become Reality

Joseph's journey in the Bible is a testament to God's unwavering presence and guidance through every hair-pin turn of life's path. From the moment Joseph received his prophetic dreams of greatness, God's hand was upon him, orchestrating events to fulfill His divine purpose. Despite facing ridicule and disbelief from his own family, Joseph held fast to the dreams God had placed in his heart. Through every trial and setback, from being sold into slavery by his brothers to being falsely accused and imprisoned, Joseph remained steadfast in his faith, trusting in God's plan for his life (Genesis 37).

I have experienced words of prophecy over my life through men and women of God. Even though I trust God to speak through these people, I often don't understand how those promises and purposes would ever come about — especially when looking at the circumstances. I'll admit I had times when I doubted it could happen through me — for me. I was so wrapped up in my current trial or disappointment I couldn't see beyond the potential problems. I was so convinced it couldn't happen I would forget about the prophecy altogether — until it came true! I'll share more later, but know this: God knew how it would come together all along. And He knows it for you, too.

Joseph did not understand how his dreams would manifest and didn't foresee the challenges he would face before they were revealed. However, despite the hard road, sacrifices, and obstacles, he eventually went from the pit to the palace.

Even in the depths of despair, God never abandoned Joseph. Instead, He used each trial as a stepping stone towards victory. Joseph's unwavering faith and integrity ultimately led him to a position of power and influence in Egypt, where he played a pivotal role in saving his family and the entire nation from famine. Through God's grace and Joseph's obedience, what was intended for harm was transformed into a triumph of redemption and restoration (Genesis 43-45). Joseph's story is a powerful reminder that no matter the obstacles we face, God is always with us, guiding us toward victory and fulfilling the dreams He has planted in our hearts.

Maybe becoming a media mogul like Oprah isn't your dream. Perhaps writing a book or going back to school to enhance your knowledge and job skills resonates more with you. Whatever your dream looks like, it's essential to recognize that God has placed that dream in your heart, and it's His desire to see those dreams become a reality. Are you starting to remember what God has spoken into your life or over your family? Perhaps because of finances, lack of support, or direction, you just can't see how all of the working parts will fit together to crank out your victory. Or you might be walking in a well-lit part of the path, able to see the people, opportunities, and God's provision leading the way to your purpose. Wherever you are in your Dream Journey, acknowledging God in your life and surrendering your will for His will inevitably lead you to accomplish your vision. When you get to those sections of rocky, uneven road, rain is pouring down on you, and the terrain is threatening a mudslide, grab the Rock and ride it out.

When you dare to dream and embrace your future with open arms, there's no limit to what you can achieve. Now that we've thought through it let's get to it! Just know that it may come with some twists and turns and detours from Point A to Point B like it did with Joseph.

Your palace awaits, and discovering your purpose is the first step in understanding your calling and giftings. Let's explore how God uniquely made you to reach your dreams.

7 Game-Changing Habits for Transformational Outcomes

Internal Preparation

1. Eliminate one non-essential task from your schedule.

   Benefit: Free up time and mental energy for activities that align with your goals, leading to increased productivity and focus.

2. Commit to practicing positive affirmations regularly.

   Benefit: Cultivate a mindset of self-belief and empowerment, boosting confidence and motivation to pursue your goals with conviction.

3. Swap unhealthy snacks for nutritious options.

   Benefit: Making small adjustments to your snack choices can significantly impact your energy levels and concentration throughout the day.

4. Trade passive entertainment for active pursuits.

   Benefit: Engage in activities that stimulate your mind and body, fostering personal growth, creativity, and fulfillment.

5. Focus on single-tasking instead of multitasking.

   Benefit: Enhance productivity and efficiency by dedicating your full attention to one task at a time, leading to better results and reduced stress.

6. Surround yourself with positive role models.

   Benefit: Gain inspiration, guidance, and support from individuals who embody qualities and values that align with your aspirations, accelerating your growth and success.

7. Take full accountability and ditch excuses.

   Benefit: Empower yourself to take control of your life and decisions, leading to greater ownership of your actions and outcomes and, ultimately, progress towards your goals.

DREAM COME TRUE

Oprah Winfrey

Born into poverty in rural Mississippi in 1954, Oprah faced numerous challenges throughout her early life, including poverty, abuse, and discrimination. However, she refused to let her circumstances define her. Instead, she relied on her intelligence, resilience, and determination to chart a path to success.

Oprah made her acting debut in 1985 as "Sofia" in Steven Spielberg's *The Color Purple*[2], for which she received both Academy Award and Golden Globe nominations. Oprah's breakthrough came when her local Chicago talk show went into national syndication and became television's highest-ranked talk show. *The Oprah Winfrey Show* showcased her authenticity, empathy, and ability to connect with audiences as she tackled a wide range of topics, from personal growth and spirituality to social issues and current events.

Beyond her talk show, Oprah expanded her media empire to include a successful magazine, a television network *(OWN: Oprah Winfrey Network)*, and various philanthropic endeavors. She has also received numerous awards and honors for her contributions to the entertainment industry and advocacy work.[3]

Oprah has used her platform throughout her career to uplift and inspire millions worldwide. She has championed causes related to education, literacy, women's empowerment, and racial justice, leveraging her influence to effect positive change on a global scale.

> "Doing the best at this moment puts you in the best place for the next moment."[4]
>
> *Oprah*

Oprah Winfrey's journey is a powerful example of resilience, determination, and the transformative power of self-belief. Despite facing significant obstacles, she remained steadfast in pursuing her dreams and worked tirelessly to achieve her goals. Today, Oprah is not only one of the most influential figures in media and entertainment but also a symbol of hope and inspiration for countless individuals striving to make their own dreams a reality.

WEEK 2

Discover Your Purpose

Unveil Your True Calling

"My 50th birthday made me examine my life. So I told my husband I was going to start a rock band." *Nancy L.*

"I remember this feeling of wanting to be a doctor when I was younger." *Carl A.*

"Never in a million years did I think that at the age of 24 I would have achieved my biggest and wildest dream – to work at the hospital I was treated at as a child/teenager. It's amazing and crazy and awesome and I'm SO excited!" *Montana B[5].*

Have you ever pondered, "What on earth am I here for?" It's a question that resonates deeply with many of us at various points in our lives. After a speaking event, a church service, or even personal conversations, I've encountered countless individuals wrestling with this question. Many have dreams and aspirations but struggle to discern the purpose behind their existence. Some forget all about their earlier desires when life's demands take over, only to rediscover them at a crossroads or when a blind curve throws them off course. Often, God will use the unexpected to deliver His unparalleled purpose into focus.

Carl Allamby faced a dilemma. His auto-repair business, which he started when he was only nineteen years old, had grown into two bustling shops with eleven employees. However, despite his success, Allamby felt restless and unfulfilled. Can you relate to feeling unsettled even when others may see you as a success? Carl thought about expanding his business to satisfy this yearning, so he decided to pursue a bachelor's degree in business management. This is where God introduced Carl's true purpose for his future.

The business management curriculum required biology credits. During the first class, Carl was reminded of a long-forgotten childhood dream: becoming a doctor. Growing up in a disadvantaged African American neighborhood in East Cleveland, Ohio, Allamby faced numerous obstacles and low expectations. His school lacked advanced science courses, and being a *brain* would have been dangerous for him in his neighborhood, so he let go of that desire. Then, at almost forty, God steered him back to that dream by allowing him to feel unsatisfied with his situation. Then He reintroduced that exciting, fresh feeling of wanting something else — something more. Have you felt that pull toward an idea you left behind? Or maybe what made you happy in one stage of life has you unfulfilled recently.

When you were younger, you may have considered attending college, learning a skill, starting a company, making a million bucks overnight, or losing 30 pounds in 30 days. With time, you realize none of these things happen quickly or easily. Even if you have achieved great success in some areas, there may come a day when you wake up and realize that although you have what you set out to attain, there's still something lacking.

A feeling of dissatisfaction doesn't necessarily mean you took a wrong turn; it may just be a sign that God wants you to *want* again — dream again. If you are feeling antsy, unfulfilled, and unsettled, ask the Lord to show you what He has in mind for you. The proficiencies and desire to diagnose and remedy patients come from the same root qualities and motivations that made Carl Allamby's auto-repair business a success. Early in Carl's life, God gave him the drive to identify and fix broken things — first cars, then people. As you seek out your purpose, don't be surprised if it involves a craving, talent, or experience you already possess.

Discovering your purpose is not simply about identifying a career path or achieving personal goals; it's about understanding the unique role you were created to fulfill in God's grand design.

Each of us has been endowed with specific gifts, talents, and passions, tailor-made for the purpose that God has ordained for our lives. By embracing and cultivating these gifts, we unlock our full potential and pave the way for extraordinary growth and success.

As you step into the fullness of your purpose and operate in the gifts that God has given you, you'll find yourself growing and thriving in ways you never imagined possible. Opportunities will abound, relationships will blossom into something more meaningful, and obstacles will crumble beneath your feet.

The dream that once seemed distant or unattainable will draw nearer with each step you take in faith. Remember, God's plans for you are good, and He delights in seeing His children prosper.

> *"Every good thing given and every perfect gift is from above, coming down from the Father of lights, with whom there is no variation or shifting shadow."*
> — James 1:17 (NASB)

This week, we'll delve into the journey of self-discovery and faith, exploring practical steps to unveil our true calling and boldly into the purpose God has prepared for us. Through prayer, reflection, and seeking God's guidance, we'll embark on a transformative journey to uncover the unique destiny that awaits each of us. Get ready to discover your purpose and embrace the extraordinary adventure God has in store for you!

When you align yourself with your purpose and operate in the gifts God has bestowed upon you, remarkable things happen. It's as if the puzzle pieces start falling into place, clicking together with a satisfying finality. Your path becomes more apparent and defined like a beam of light guides you forward. You experience deep fulfillment and satisfaction when you're in sync with your purpose. Your actions become purposeful, each step intentional and guided by an unmistakable trail of divine breadcrumbs leading you closer to your destiny. What an amazing feeling!

True success goes beyond just personal achievements and accumulating wealth. Instead, it involves being driven by a deeper purpose and recognizing that we are all part of something bigger.

In his book, *The Purpose Driven Life: What On Earth Am I Here For,* Rick Warren wrote, "You cannot fulfill God's purposes for your life while focusing on your own plans."[6] Purpose-driven success means evolving, making an impact, and leaving a positive footprint on the world. To truly find significance, we must move past survival and self-centered goals and instead understand our larger role in fulfilling God's purpose for our lives.

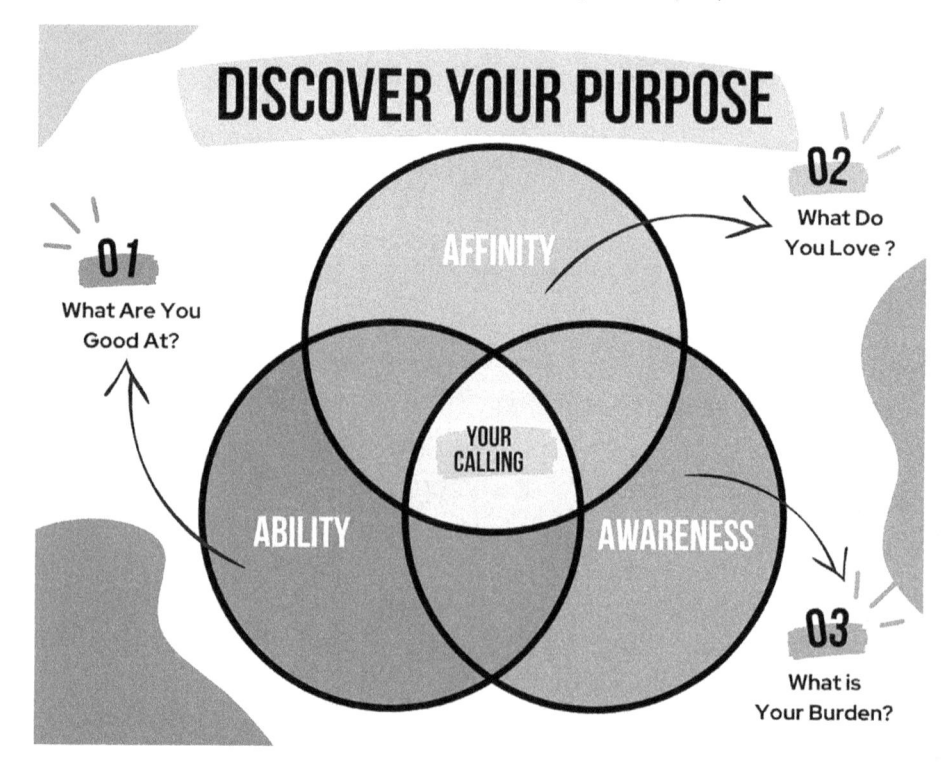

DISCOVER YOUR PURPOSE

01 What Are You Good At?

02 What Do You Love?

03 What is Your Burden?

- AFFINITY
- ABILITY
- AWARENESS
- YOUR CALLING

Profit v Purpose

In seeking your purpose, be careful not to answer only the questions of what you're good at and enjoy. Look within, yes, but also look around. What does the world need from you? Ask God to shift your focus from individual success to a greater understanding of how all the pieces fit together in your journey towards a fulfilling life.

My family was very poor when I was growing up. We often didn't know where our next meal would come from, but we trusted God. We believed so wholly in the Lord's provision that our family began an outreach to rescue young men and women from addiction and life on the streets. At a time when we struggled to feed our own family, we added mouths to the mix. And somehow, there was enough for us and for the strangers we invited to the table. Ultimate satisfaction begins with unflinching sacrifice.

My family had four kids: my brother, two sisters, and me. Hand-me-downs was all I knew. There was no back-to-school shopping or special dress for class picture day. But I didn't even know we were poor until some mean girl pointed it out when my outfit for photos wasn't up to par. Looking back, I don't think we went to the mall for a new school outfit until I was in high school.

> **Ultimate satisfaction begins with unflinching sacrifice.**

When I turned seventeen, I planned to attend college in Tulsa, Oklahoma. I was so excited I got a significant head start on packing my belongings with my sights set on my grand adventure. *It's finally my turn!* One evening, my dad came into my room and motioned me to sit beside him.

"Your mom and I cannot afford to send you to college. We have so many mouths to feed. We're so sorry, Rosalinda."

I felt like I'd been kicked in the stomach. I was heartbroken. I have always understood my family's call to reach other people and help them rise up to the purpose God has for them. It was the story of my young life to feed them from my plate, clothe them from my closet, and trade my bed for the floor so someone else could rest. I am not trying to sound like a martyr; this is just how I was raised — I was born into my family's purpose, even before I came to recognize it as part of my own. In this moment of disappointment, I was inspired to find a solution to the struggles and practical needs that came with the family ministry.

Discovering Purpose in Painful Moments

My hopes of going to college could have died before my tears had a chance to dry from my cheeks; instead, I decided to not be upset with God or my parents. I determined to do something about my circumstances. I locked myself in my room and devised a plan: *I would become a millionaire.*

Problem solved.

I opened my first little shop at the super flea market, renting the space for $60 a month. My business plan involved buying used stuffed animals at the Goodwill across the street and selling them at my table. The process was thrilling. Even before I sold my first item, I was hooked on retail. Something inside me was doing cartwheels with every price tag I attached and every sign I put up. When you're in the zone, even the monotony is exciting. I took great pride in the meticulous inspection I gave each fuzzy bear and pink elephant before choosing it for my business. *My* business — a venture I realized was not likely to earn me a million bucks before I was white-haired and putting my teeth in a cup. But I was determined. All I needed was a better product.

Count the cost before you decide.

Impressed by my grit and grind, my dad sat down with me to encourage me. In my mind, the conversation over leftover empanadas was the mark of my first official business meeting. I wondered if it could be claimed as a tax write-off. The wheels were spinning.

Dad told me about a Jewish guy he knew in New York who was a wholesaler of silk ties. Most men wore neckties in the nineties, but I wondered how

I would make that pitch. Then he suggested I test the waters: take a box of assorted neckties to dealerships and stores and see what bites. So I did. I made my list of prospective customers and saw them all in one day. I had the right product, but I needed more inventory. *How can I do this, but bigger?* I needed some guidance.

> *"Without counsel plans fail, but with many advisers they succeed."*
> — Proverbs 15:22 (ESV)

Remember, I wasn't even eighteen yet, but I understood the value of wise counsel. I discussed my ideas with entrepreneurial women and couples from our church, and one of them introduced me to the concept of opening a kiosk in the local mall. I talked to my parents about it and they were supportive, but with a reminder: "Keep in mind that you are the only employee. You can't have a sick day or vacation time, and you'll be putting in eighty-five hours a week. Count the cost before you decide."

I considered the sacrifice, worked out a plan, and at seventeen years old, I signed my first lease at Chesterfield Towne Center.

Dream Principle #1

Listen To Grow

Listening is the cornerstone of growth. When we open our ears and minds to the wisdom around us, we unlock countless opportunities for personal and professional development.

I needed a loan to get started, so I went to the bank and borrowed $3000. I thought, *My God, I hope I can pay this back!* I got my deposit and first months rent for the kiosk, a little sign to attract customers, and some inventory. I was open for business! Within my first year, I had made over six figures!

I had an idea, I prayed and got great advice, I made a plan, and did the work. And there was plenty of work. Nothing could have prepared me for all of the extras like opening and closing the store, cleaning the store, mopping the store, and doing the paperwork. There was So. Much. Paperwork. Father's Day and Christmas were especially booming. I worked over 125 hours the week of Christmas. After expenses, I still didn't have enough money for college, but, boy, did I get the best hands-on experience.

Even with that initial success, I knew I was green and needed to surround myself with people who had already been where I wanted to go, so I attended trade shows in Las Vegas. Wholesalers from all over the world fill this along with wholesalers from all over the world. and could get from A-Z quicker by learning from the mastery and mistakes of other people. I was a hungry teen, eager to soak in every bit I could from these fifty and sixty-year-olds.

This was truly a pivotal point in my business career. I owned a business, but I was too young to rent a car or get a hotel room, so I brought my mom, Carmen. As we walked into the beautiful lobby of Caesar's Palace, Mom said emphatically, "Sin de juegos de azar." No gambling. As she checked in, a six-inch flashing button made to look like a poker chip caught my eye. On it was the word "Collect" in gold letters. So, I reached across the counter and pushed the button. BAM! Seventy-five dollars shot out! My mom's head whipped around, "I said, 'No gambling,' Rosalinda."

With a big grin, I joked, "I'm not gambling. I'm col-lec-tiiiing." I figured I would buy a souvenir at one of the hotel gift shops — maybe a Caesar's Palace t-shirt. I excitedly told the man behind the counter that I didn't have to gamble to win. He laughed and told me I couldn't even buy a keychain for only $75. Reality check. I hoped the rest of my trip would be more profitable.

The next morning, I began networking. I was eager to hear stories from the salespeople, develop wholesale connections, and learn the keys to others' success. Listening is the cornerstone of growth. Putting away pride and remaining willing to receive guidance has helped me advance in my purpose and strategically move up the ladder faster.

Once you know what you want to do, you have to discover what it takes to get there. Knowing what you are good at and recognizing what you are passionate about will help make your dreams a reality. Understanding your strengths is crucial. When you excel in something naturally, enjoyment often follows. While success demands perseverance, leveraging your innate talents can ease the journey.

Passion and proficiency don't always align perfectly. Discerning between the two is vital to avoid mismatched career and life paths. *(see the Purpose Worksheet: Passions and Proficiency in Appendix)*

Balancing both strengths and passions ensures a fulfilling career path where talent and enthusiasm converge for optimal success.

STRENGTH

- 🚀 **Natural ability:** Efficient performance in specific tasks or situations.
- 🚀 **Knowledge-based:** Easily grasp and build on the subject matter.
- 🚀 **Recognition:** Others acknowledge and appreciate your abilities.

PASSION

- 🚀 **Skill level:** Proficiency isn't a prerequisite.
- 🚀 **Interest-based:** Inherent desire to learn and engage.
- 🚀 **Intrinsic motivation:** Inner satisfaction outweighs external rewards.

Dream Principle #2

Trust God

When we trust God's guidance and timing, we discover the courage to wholeheartedly chase our dreams. By letting go of our fears and doubts, we embrace His plan for our lives, finding hope and fulfillment in the journey.

Lessons Learned in the Wilderness

Moses was born into a world of oppression but was chosen by God for a great purpose. At a pivotal moment, Moses encountered God at the burning bush while tending sheep (Exodus 3:1-10). Despite being raised in Pharaoh's palace, when God called him to lead the Israelites out of slavery in Egypt, Moses hesitated. He doubted his capabilities and questioned whether he was the right person for such a monumental task. Moses felt disconnected from his people and uncertain about his identity and purpose. It's in this wilderness experience that God unveiled His plan for Moses and promised to lead the way, night and day.

> *"And the Lord went before them by day in a pillar of cloud to lead them along the way, and by night in a pillar of fire to give them light, that they might travel by day and by night."*
>
> — Exodus 13:21 (ESV)

The journey out of Egypt was not easy, as Moses faced numerous trials. He had to confront Pharaoh, experience miraculous plagues from God, and lead the Israelites through a harsh wilderness. One significant moment was when God parted the Red Sea. Despite the overwhelming situation,

Moses trusted in God's guidance. He stretched out his hand, causing the sea to open and allowing the people to pass through safely (Exodus 14).

Throughout it all, Moses learned to let go of control and put his trust in God. His unwavering faith continues to inspire generations, reminding us that God remains faithful no matter what challenges we may face.

Like Moses, you may be in a season of uncertainty, struggling with questions about your worth. When God reveals your purpose and directs you toward the people you will impact, trust Him to provide everything you will need to accomplish what He's called you to do. Do not limit yourself or let anyone else hold you back. It's time to kick down the doors that have been locking you out. Today's the day to break every barrier to your dream; knowing God's "yes" is the only approval you need.

> "Sometimes it is the people no one imagines anything of who do the things that no one can imagine."
>
> Alan Turing
> *The Imitation Game*

7 Game-Changing Habits for Transformational Outcomes

Pinpoint Your Purpose

1. **Seek God's Will in Prayer.**

   Benefit: You will learn more about who you are by getting to know your Creator more intimately. God will reveal His plan and guide you in the path He ordained.

2. **Study God's Word for Guidance.**

   Benefit: You will receive guidance and wisdom. God's Word will give insight into His character, promises, and purposes for humanity and clarify your role in that plan.

3. **Listen to the Holy Spirit.**

   Benefit: The Holy Spirit serves as our counselor and guide. Tune into the voice of the Holy Spirit as He convicts and directs. Be attentive to His promptings and trust His leading as you navigate your journey of purpose discovery.

4. **Serve in Your Gifts for God's Glory.**

   Benefit: Identify and use your spiritual gifts to serve others and advance God's kingdom. When we align our gifts to God's will, we experience a deep sense of fulfillment and purpose.

5. **Walk in Faith and Obedience.**

   Benefit: Be willing to surrender your own desires and preferences to God's leading, knowing that His ways are higher than our ways.

6. **Heed Counsel from Fellow Believers.**

   Benefit: Surround yourself with believers who can offer wisdom, encouragement, and accountability. Guided by Biblical insights, you will be strengthened and protected.

7. **Stay Anchored in God's Love and Truth.**

   Benefit: Your value is not determined by accomplishments but by your identity as a beloved child of God. Find security and confidence in God's promises, knowing He has a purpose for your life.

DREAM COME TRUE

Shirley Chisholm

"Unbought and Unbossed."

That was the campaign slogan of 1972 presidential candidate Shirley Chisholm. Long before Carol Moseley Braun, Barack Obama, and Hillary Clinton made their historic runs for the presidency, Shirley Chisholm paved the way as both the first woman and the first African American to seek the nomination of a major political party in the United States.

The daughter of immigrants, Shirley Chisholm was born into poverty in Brooklyn, New York. After graduating with a Bachelor of Arts, she taught in her church nursery school while studying for her Master's at Colombia.

Then Chisholm turned to politics becoming the first Black woman to be elected to the United States Congress in 1968 before throwing her hat in the ring as a potential candidate for the presidency.

"If they don't give you a seat at the table, bring a folding chair."
Shirley Chisholm

While her presidential bid was unsuccessful, she laid the foundations for those who would come after her, teaching them that anything was possible.

WEEK 3

Defy Limiting Beliefs

Break Barriers and Embrace Potential

Are you holding your dreams hostage? Are you the unsuspecting jailkeeper of your own dreams? Picture it: your dreams are like eager prisoners, ready to break free, but you, in your unwitting role, are holding the key to their cell. How did this happen? Well, it's like a scene from a suspenseful drama. You're on the brink of daring to dream, feeling the excitement bubble up within you, when suddenly, the weight of your responsibilities crashes down on your enthusiasm. Your job, your family, your finances – they all clamor for your attention, drowning out the whispers of your aspirations. And before you know it, your dreams are locked up tight behind the bars of self-doubt and excuses. But fear not because you hold the power to set them free and unleash their boundless potential. It's time to stage the ultimate jailbreak and reclaim your right to dream big!

It's easy to get caught up in the trap of disqualifying yourself, your dreams, and your opportunities. And many of your anticipated difficulties are valid. You aren't likely to get from your imagined success to actually living it without struggles and setbacks. My family sure had plenty of them.

My father migrated to the United States from Puerto Rico, and my mother from Mexico. They both had an eighth-grade education; my mother didn't speak English. We had no money for groceries and relied on prayer to bring food to the table. Faith, Food Stamps, and enormous blocks of orange-yellow government cheese kept us in cheese sandwiches and bland **Kix** cereal during our school years.

I barely graduated high school. When it came time to further my education, I didn't even know how to fill out the forms to get student aid. There was no smooth path from where I stood to the life I wanted to have. It was not easy, but we learned how to work hard. My parents brought us up serving the Lord. While there were countless struggles, the word ***impossible*** was not in Mom and Dad's vocabulary — and it isn't in mine.

Perhaps your upbringing mirrors my own, where every opportunity was hard-won, and every inch forward felt like a victory. Or maybe your start was different, surrounded by cheerleaders and supporters, leaving you wondering now why you're not farther along. Each of us has walked a unique path shaped by our own experiences, circumstances, and responses. But one thing remains constant – God has planted a dream within each of us, a spark waiting to ignite into something extraordinary. It's all about mindset.

It's time to silence the doubts and fears that hold us back and embrace the motivating truth that it's right to dream, it's okay to succeed, and being who we were created to be is a position endorsed by God Almighty. So, let's cheer ourselves on, knowing that the journey ahead may be challenging, but the destination is worth every step. It's time to dust off those dreams, stand tall, and boldly step into the greatness that awaits us. Breaking barriers and embracing our full potential is a theme deeply woven into the fabric of the Bible, exemplified by the story of Joshua and the walls of Jericho.

In the book of Joshua, we find the Israelites facing a seemingly insurmountable obstacle — the fortified city of Jericho, with its towering walls and formidable defenses. From a human perspective, the task of conquering such a city appeared impossible. That's why Joshua embraced a different perspective — the Lord's.

God gave Joshua a clear command —

"Walk around the city. Have all the men of war go around the city once. Do this for six days. Seven religious leaders will carry seven rams' horns. They will walk in front of the special box of the agreement. Then on the seventh day you will walk around the city seven times. And the religious leaders will blow horns. When you hear the long sound of the ram's horn, all the people should call out with a loud noise. The wall of the city will fall to the ground. And then all the people will all go in the city."
— Joshua 6:3-5 (NLV)

Joshua led the Israelites in this unconventional strategy, and they witnessed a miraculous display of God's power.

"On the seventh day they got up early at the rising of the sun. They walked around the city in the same way, but on that day they walked around the city seven times. The seventh time, when the religious leaders blew their horns, Joshua said to the people, 'Call out! For the Lord has given you the city.' [...] When the people heard the sound of the horns, they called out even louder. And the wall fell to the ground. All the people went straight in and took the city."

— Joshua 6:15-16, 20 (NLV)

One week before, the city of Jericho appeared impenetrable. Winning seemed impossible, and the plan was impractical. Still, God gave the Israelites the victory, proving again that it ain't over til the Lord says it's over. That applies to whatever is trying to keep you out or trap you in.

You can overcome even the most formidable obstacles with unwavering faith and God's guidance. Just as the Israelites had to confront the walls of Jericho, you must confront the barriers in your life. If self-doubt, fear of failure, or societal expectations block you, trust in God's plan and open yourself up to limitless potential and boundless opportunities.

Embracing your full potential means acknowledging your innate talents, strengths, and unique gifts. We are each capable of far more than we often give ourselves credit for. By nurturing our strengths and stepping into our authenticity, we can unleash our full potential and unlock opportunities for growth and success.

Mother Cabrini

Saint Frances Xavier Cabrini was a remarkable figure known for her tireless dedication to serving the poor and marginalized, particularly immigrants. "Mother Cabrini" encountered discrimination and prejudice in late 19th-century New York City because she was a woman and Italian. Still, she never let it stop her from helping others.

Despite the obstacles, Cabrini created charities and hospitals working diligently to care for Italian immigrants who came to the city for a better life. Her unwavering determination and deep faith motivated those around her to do the same. She is still inspiring people to this day.

> **Dreams divinely inspired are not beneficial only to the dreamer.**

I recently saw the movie *Cabrini* on International Women's Day.[7] It moved me like nothing I've seen in years. I stood up at the end and joined in the standing ovation. I even donated a hundred dollars to help get the film in more theaters nationwide. That is how convinced I am that others will feel just as empowered after seeing what this woman fought through to accomplish what she believed in. If she could do it, I could reach one more time, dream once more, and make my life count — no matter who tries to get in my way.

This Catholic nun fought the establishment and won, but not immediately. Cabrini pleaded with the cardinal year after year to open the necessary doors so she could get permission to leave Italy. Finally, she got an audience with the pope and set out on a brutal journey across the sea to help those in greatest need. You see, Cabrini's desires weren't about her.

Dreams divinely inspired are not beneficial only to the dreamer.

When she reached her destination, Mother Cabrini rescued children living in the sewage systems underground. She recognized the challenges faced by these little ones, many of whom were orphaned or came from impoverished families struggling to make a living in a new country. In response, Mother Cabrini established orphanages and schools specifically tailored to meet the needs of Italian immigrant children.

Cabrini relied on her strong faith, determination, and resourcefulness to open these homes, risking her own life and battling an illness that would later take her life. Despite facing financial challenges and resistance from some neighborhoods, she tirelessly sought donations. Rallying support from the community, Cabrini collaborated with local authorities and charitable organizations to secure the necessary resources and permissions to establish and operate the orphanages. Soon, requests for her to open schools came from all over the world to Frances Cabrini. She made twenty-three trans-Atlantic crossings and established 67 schools, hospitals, and orphanages in Europe, Central and South America, and throughout the United States.[8]

Mother Cabrini dared to dream. You may not open orphanages all over the world, but your dream's fulfillment can meet a need in the world around you. In fact, it must.

If you are marching around a barricaded treasure, those walls will only crumble at the command of the Lord and for His purposes. God is giving you the capacity to reach the place He is sending you. The *hoping* is your responsibility. The trusting God part is up to you, just like it was with Joshua demolishing obstacles, Mother Cabrini's developing orphanages, and Esther when she spoke up and delivered the outsiders.

Queen Esther, a fearless Jewish woman in Persian exile, faced grave danger as her people were threatened by a wicked plot. With determination and courage, she risked her life to plead for their safety before the king. Her actions saved countless lives and serve as a reminder of the power of selflessness and making a difference in the face of adversity (Esther 2-8).

Mother Cabrini and Queen Esther share several remarkable similarities that underscore their enduring legacy of courage, compassion, and unwavering faith.

First, Mother Cabrini and Queen Esther were ordinary women who were in extraordinary circumstances. Both allowed themselves to be in unfamiliar surroundings to save their people; Cabrini, the Italian immigrant children, and Esther, the Jewish people.

Second, both women displayed remarkable courage in the face of adversity. Mother Cabrini fearlessly embarked on perilous journeys to establish schools, hospitals, and orphanages, often facing harsh opposition and daunting obstacles. Similarly, Queen Esther risked her life to intercede on behalf of her people, bravely approaching the king to plead for their deliverance from impending doom.

Third, both Mother Cabrini and Queen Esther exemplified the power of selflessness and compassion. Mother Cabrini dedicated her life to serving the marginalized and disadvantaged, tirelessly advocating for the welfare of immigrants and orphaned children. Likewise, Queen Esther demonstrated extraordinary concern for her people, willingly placing herself in harm's way to secure their safety and well-being.

Last, both women's stories serve as timeless reminders of the profound impact one individual can have on the world. Through their courage, compassion, and unwavering faith, Mother Cabrini and Queen Esther transformed lives, inspired countless others to dare to dream, and left an indelible mark on history.

Just like Esther, we have the power to break free from the limitations that try to keep us small. She defied the status quo by stepping up to save her people, the Jews, from destruction, even though it meant risking her own life. Despite the odds stacked against her, she used her influence to make a difference.

Breaking barriers and embracing our full potential is like kicking down the doors that hold us back from living our best lives. It's about saying, "No more!" to the doubts and fears that tell us we're not capable enough. Some blocks come down with one determined decision, like the blow of a battering ram. Others may have been built high and thick throughout your life and need to be chiseled away until the foundation of lies cracks and crumbles. Either way, the demolition begins when you commit to doing whatever is necessary to move forward. That's when you can construct something amazing.

"Just keep swimming."

Dory, *Finding Nemo*

7 Game-Changing Habits for Transformational Outcomes

Make Small Changes

1. Give Up Excessive Social Media Scrolling.

   Benefit: Improved concentration, reduced stress, and increased knowledge from reading or pursuing interests.

2. Change Morning Routine.

   Benefit: Exercise and Prayer increases energy and focus and decreases anxiety and sets a positive tone for the day.

3. Give Up Unhealthy Eating Habits.

   Benefit: Better physical health, improved mood, and sustained levels of energy and supports overall well-being..

4. Change Bedtime Routine.

Benefit: Relaxation techniques such as deep breathing or gentle stretching result in better quality sleep, reduced insomnia, and overall improved health.

5. Stop Procrastinating.

Benefit: Time management increases productivity, reduces stress, and a sense of accomplishment. Prioritizing tasks helps focus on what truly matters.

6. Declutter and Organize.

Benefit: Improved focus, reduced mental clutter, and increased efficiency. A tidy space promotes clear thinking and minimizes distractions.

7. Resist Negativity.

Benefit: Positive, self-talk improves self-esteem, reduces anxiety, and greater resilience. Positive affirmations foster a healthy mindset and reinforce self-worth.

DREAM COME TRUE

Nick Vujicic

Nick Vujicic was born without arms or legs. But that didn't stop him from reaching his dreams. Because children with tetra-amelia syndrome have such serious medical problems, most are stillborn or die shortly after birth. Nick is an extraordinary individual who has touched millions with his incredible story of perseverance and determination.

Nick's rare congenital disorder, causing him immense challenges. Nick was bullied throughout his school years but turns that pain into the path to success for children and adults alike as he travels to schools, churches, and governments advocating for anti-bullying initiatives all over the globe.

The title of Nick's best-selling book says it all —

"Life Without Limits: Inspiration for a Ridiculously Good Life."

Nick considers himself to be someone who does have a ridiculously good life sharing the message of Jesus Christ through his non-profit, "Life Without Limbs." His school curriculum, "Attitude Is Altitude," empowers students with positive values and resilience.

Nick's impact goes beyond physical limitations, encouraging others to embrace life's challenges with courage and hope. Nick knows adversity firsthand, making his work all the more meaningful.

Vujicic has consistently shown that there is pretty much nothing he can't do. Nick says, "If God can use a man without arms and legs to be His hands and feet, then He will certainly use any willing heart."

> "Don't let your limitations define you. Let your determination redefine your limitations."
>
> *Nick Vujicic*

WEEK 4

Develop Resilience

Transforming Setbacks into Opportunities

"Help! I've fallen, and I can't get up!" You probably remember that phrase if you were around in the late '80s. It became a cult classic in 1989 by a poorly-acted commercial for *Life Alert*, a medical alert button for senior citizens who can't reach the phone in a health emergency. Still, the catchphrase took off in an unexpected direction, appearing on t-shirts, bumper stickers, and novelty records, and was repeated *ad nauseam* by stand-up comedians. Writers for *The Fresh Prince of Bel Air*, *The Golden Girls*, and *Roseanne* all had their fun with it.[9] A sampling of Mrs. Fletcher's cry for help even landed in a Swedish progressive rock song in 2002.[10] The phrase, created by Edith Fore, the actress who played the helpless lady, is a registered trademark of the company over thirty years later, the product grossing over $44 million.

"Help! I've fallen, and I can't get up!"

The line wasn't meant to be funny. There's nothing humorous about an older person taking a spill. There's nothing fun about a broken hip — or broken hope.

There are many types of falls, many ways to fall, and an equal number of responses after a fall. Have you ever felt like you've tripped up — spiritually, emotionally, physically —and you don't know how you'll ever get steady?

Perhaps there was a failure in attempting to start a business, the end of a relationship, or a disappointing dream launch. The reality is that we all experience setbacks.

Failures and botched opportunities will propel you toward your future or hinder you from lifting off. It depends on what you do next. How do you view the slowing progress — Delay? Or *Doom*?

Popcorn and Persistence

Let me take you back to the movies. On a movie date night with my wonderful husband Carlos, we saw *The Pursuit of Happyness*.[11] The film stars Will Smith as Chris Gardner, a single dad struggling to escape poverty and homelessness.

In the early 1980s, Gardner could not afford rent after his wife left him, forcing him to live on the streets with his young son, Christopher Jr. Despite these dire circumstances, Gardner refused to give up on his dreams of a better life for them. He took on various odd jobs to make ends meet, including working as a medical equipment salesman. Chris faced rejection at every turn. Like anyone, he had moments of self-doubt when his frustration got the better of him. Sure, when everything and everyone turned against him, he battled feelings of inadequacy and guilt as a father. But he kept going. He identified every injustice and brutal turn of events as nothing more significant than a *delay*. He refused to be defeated. His family would not doomed.

Halfway through the movie, I'm already in tears over the beautiful strength of this man. I'm a sucker for a good underdog story of overcoming through impossible odds. The two Christophers slept in parks, on a rough bathroom floor at a railway station, and ate in soup kitchens. Then, after a year of homelessness with his toddler (depicted as older in the movie), Chris finally caught a break.

Gardner secured an unpaid internship at a prestigious stock brokerage firm despite having no formal education or experience in finance. He worked tirelessly, often sleeping under his desk after everyone else had gone home. His work ethic, determination, and ingenuity caught the attention of the higher-ups, and Chris was offered a full-time position as a stockbroker. Chris Gardner later founded a successful brokerage firm, Gardner, Rich, & Co. The dad bathing his child in gas station bathrooms is worth over $60 million today.

When you encounter setbacks, do you see them as signs you're destined to fail, or do you interpret those struggles as a delay? Do you give up, or do you catch your breath, investigate causes, and create solutions for the next run at your dream?

Setbacks are merely obstacles in the grand scheme of your journey toward success. How you perceive them will determine if you drop to your knees for strength or throw up your hands in defeat. The choice belongs to the goal-setter in those moments.

As children of God, we can be encouraged that if we fail or fall, God will lift us up and set us right. Let me drill this into your thinking and understanding — Give God the glory for the success and gratitude in the struggle, and He will secure your goals with every step you take.

By approaching failures with a resilient mindset and a determination to keep moving forward, you will rise above adversity and emerge tougher and more prepared for the next phase of your journey. Don't be surprised if God reintroduces a forgotten pleasure or resource down the road.

In 2006, Carlos attended a training convention of the Utah Bankers Association. Bankers and mortgage brokers worldwide gathered to learn how to help people pay off their mortgages early. I was there with him, surrounded by successful business people. I thought, *Why in the world* am I here? What am I doing with my life? I love supporting my husband, but I wondered when I would get a chance at my own dreams. These conversations with myself were becoming more frequent.

Standing on the side of a row at the bottom floor of the venue, I struck up a conversation with the man standing next to me. I'll never forget he was kind of artsy looking; *Definitely not from Utah,* I thought. He wore a green army jacket instead of the typical banker three-piece suit. His scraggly beard and carefree attitude gave off a California vibe. Sure enough, that's where he was from. I discovered that the conference creator was a young CEO and my new friend's client. He shared with me that this brilliant young man had created a system to help people get out of debt earlier, but no one knew about it.

The idea sat dormant because the CEO was so busy with the day-to-day demands of his business that he forgot, or no longer made time for his absolute dream to expand and cast a vision for the future. This guy appeared amid my crisis of purpose, and I started spilling my angst all over him. This personal consultant temporarily became my personal consultant.

He asked all the usual questions: *Where are you from? What do you do?* When I described the responsibilities of running my family's non-profit, the weight of financial concerns that go along with it, and how little time or energy I'm left with to do anything else, he asked another question.

"What else do you want to do?"

Hearing the question out loud put a lump in my throat. No one ever asked that. For most of my adult life, I hadn't dared ask myself what else I might want out of life. I love my work for *New Life for Adults and Youth,* helping people transform their lives through Jesus; I'm told it shows. I suppose it never occurred to anyone that I might have some secret dream hidden away inside. But God knew because He put it there. And now this stranger was asking me to declare my dream. So I did. As I shared each sector of my vision, he responded by frustrating me with one repeated question:

"So, how are you gonna do it?"

With each of my rebuttals, excuses, or hesitations, for a solid half-hour, he asked that same question. He left me nowhere to run except toward the drafting board to design a plan for my journey.

You will not believe what happened next!

Surprise Confirmations

The lights in the venue blinked off and on, signaling the time for us to take our seats. After that rocket-launching conversation, I couldn't wrangle a single coherent thought, so I was a bit distracted when the announcer was preparing to introduce the next speaker. Then a familiar name snapped me out of my delirium — "Welcome, Chris Gardner!"

What?!

It doesn't get any better. Well, actually, it did. The casual California consultant said, "Hey, Chris is a friend of mine. Would you like to meet him?"

(Maybe this trip was for me, after all.)

Whatever delay, detour, or disaster has tried to knock you off course, get back on track! The Lord is setting you up for unexpected encounters in unlikely places to tell you exactly what He assured me of that day.

If the obstacle seems too huge & overwhelming, break the boulder into bits.

Child, I am here with you. You're in my heart; you're in my thoughts; you're in my hands. Your secret dreams are inside you because I placed them there. I will equip you and provide everything and every person you need to do what I chose you to accomplish. Get up! It's time!

What is your dream?

So, how are you going to do it?

WHAT ONE THING CAN YOU DO IN THE NEXT THIRTY DAYS TO PREPARE TO LAUNCH?

- **Identify** a single behavior or way of thinking you need to quit; some distraction or waste of time.

- **Implement** a single action or mindset that focuses and moves you closer to living your dream.

You can't get to it until you get up off it and get back in it! If it all seems too overwhelming, break the boulder into bits. Remember, you don't need to know every step to take the first one. Also, setbacks are like that one family member we all have — they never call ahead. They just show up at your door.

Dream. Delay. Dream. Detour. Rinse. Repeat.

I was attending a pastor's gathering in Greenville, South Carolina, when Bishop Tony Miller spoke a word of prophecy over me. He said, "You are pregnant with twins." I sensed the Lord's presence and I understood that I would develop twin visions — two dreams. I knew that twins are not born at the exact same time. One comes after the other. One has to wait.

Delay.

At the time, my dad dreamed of seeing his life story become a movie, and that opportunity had presented itself. I have always been committed to honoring my mom and dad, and my spirit confirmed that I was to help his dream come true, and then my dream would be birthed after. Twin visions meant there would be a wait. But it also confirmed that mine was coming! I didn't realize how out of the way this detour would take me.

Immediately, I began working with scriptwriters out of Hollywood. Within a year, we were filming the motion picture **Victor.** Filming did not go smoothly or quickly and did not meet my internal timetable. I had many conversations with myself about patience, God's timing, endurance, and the unhealthy consequences of eating your feelings.

Eventually, the film was shot and edited. That's when the real work began. For the next thirty-six months, I was consumed with over one hundred flights, meeting industry people worldwide, promoting red-carpet film festivals and relaunching my father's book, which the movie was based on.

I prayed a lot during those times. I prayed and reminded myself of God's promises so that I would not lose sight of my dream while I chased hard after someone else's.

Maybe you feel the same. Do you struggle to keep hold of hope? Are there others in your life, your spouse, children, ailing parents, or a demanding boss who absorbs every drop of time and energy from your dream? And you go along because you love them (well, maybe not the boss). It's okay. God's timing is the right timing. God has a reputation for doing a swift and complete work, and He uses the resources you picked up along the detour you thought would destroy your chances! If I had gone with my plan earlier, I would've not met the people who opened the doors and made my dreams come alive much faster. There is no *yes* like God's "yes."

Living the Dream Means Surviving the Nightmare

You think your family's crazy? Let's look more closely at Joseph. Most of his life was setbacks and setups, and it was usually his own brothers doing the dirty work. From being betrayed by his own family and sold into slavery to being wrongfully imprisoned for a crime he didn't commit, Joseph's life was filled with challenges. Yet, through it all, he remained resilient and unwavering in his faith.

When Joseph told his brothers about a dream he'd had that starred him as their ruler, they showed their displeasure by selling the boy into slavery (Genesis 37:12-36). Despite this betrayal and the uncertainty of his future, Joseph remained steadfast in his faith and integrity. He served faithfully in his master's house. Being Potipher's servant did not keep him from eventually rising to a position of authority (Genesis 39:1-6). Still, he didn't get there without a few death threats and false accusations.

When Joseph rejected Potipher's wife's advances, she falsely accused him of attempted rape (Genesis 39:7-20). In the darkness of the prison cell, Joseph could have wondered if he'd gotten it wrong about the dream of ruling over his brothers. *How would he do that from jail?* Still, the dreamer maintained his trust in God and demonstrated leadership and wisdom, eventually gaining favor with the prison warden (Genesis 39:21-23).

Throughout his time in captivity, Joseph never lost sight of the dreams that God had given him as a young man. Despite his setbacks and hardships, Joseph held onto the belief that God's promises would come to fruition in his life.

Finally, Joseph's moment of triumph came when he was summoned to interpret Pharaoh's dreams, ultimately leading to his appointment as second-in-command of all Egypt (Genesis 41:14-46). Through God's providence and Joseph's resilience, he saved Egypt and his family from the devastation of famine, fulfilling the very dreams that had once caused him so much strife (Genesis 45:4-8). So, what can we learn from Joseph's example?

Forgiveness

Joseph's path was filled with betrayal from his own siblings, who sold him into slavery. Despite this tremendous pain, Joseph found it in his heart to forgive them and even offered aid during a time of famine. This story serves as a reminder that forgiveness can repair fractured relationships and release us from the weight of bitterness. When someone else's actions seem to throw your trajectory off-course, don't waste time on the cause of the calamity. Forgive and course-correct, and do it quickly. Clinging to grudges can impede our growth, but forgiveness allows us to move on with a sense of peace.

Resilience

Joseph's life took unexpected turns—from being favored by his father to becoming a slave and later being unjustly imprisoned. Yet, he remained resilient. He worked diligently in Potiphar's house and later in prison, trusting that God had a purpose for his suffering.

When pursuing our dreams, we'll encounter obstacles and setbacks. Joseph's example encourages us to stay steadfast, adapt to changing circumstances, ask for help when needed, and keep moving forward despite adversity.

Perseverance

Joseph's gift of dream interpretation propelled him to a high position in Pharaoh's court. His unshakable faith in God's direction helped him overcome obstacles and fulfill his destiny.

As we pursue our dreams, we can draw inspiration from Joseph's trust in divine guidance. Even when faced with difficult circumstances, believing God has a plan can give us the courage and determination to keep moving forward.

What is it that has held you back? Disappointments? Insecurities? Let's get real with it. We are not getting any younger, and none of us will make it out of this life alive. Waiting for any reason other than *God says so* is not waiting — it's wasting. Enough of that. Get shaking. Move forward. With baby steps or giant leaps, it's time to make this dream happen. It is your season!

Imagine this: You're at the edge of a vast ocean, the horizon stretching beyond what the eye can see. That horizon? It's your dreams, your goals, your heart's deepest desires. So often, we find ourselves cheering others on as they dive into their own seas of success, yet we hesitate to take our leap. Why? Because it's easier to believe in the courage and potential of others than in our own. You've come this far, my friend. Desiring to do something is a great start. I believe in you, and so does the Father. Do *you* believe in you?

You were crafted with greatness, designed by God with love, purpose, and an incredible destiny in mind. That's right. YOU. God didn't make a mistake when He molded you by His own hand. He poured into you a well of potential so deep that it's meant to overflow.

Now, I have a question for you that I want you to carry in your heart: Have those vibrant dreams of yours been dimmed by the trials of life? What's holding you back? Is it a chorus of past doubts, a shadow of self-doubt, or perhaps a voice whispering that your dream belongs to someone else?

Take time to reflect and pinpoint where these feelings stem from. Toss the unnecessary mental weight and begin to heal and accelerate. Are you noticing a negative echo from the past, a moment of self-doubt, or fear disguising itself as reason? Healing begins with understanding. Every one of us must say, "Search me, O God, and know my heart; test me and know my anxious thoughts" (Psalm 139:23, NLT).

Resilience isn't just about standing up again; it's about standing firm in our faith, in the knowledge that Jesus Christ has a plan for our lives that is greater than any obstacle we might face. Resilience is looking at the trials as part of the journey, not just as barriers to our destination. I've seen how obstacles, especially the mountains in my mind, can be moved when I trust in the Lord and have the support of others who share my faith and vision.

I was going through a time when I felt very down in my head. I had allowed circumstances and personal hurt to paralyze me. Certain people I had poured my heart into and trusted turned on me, forgetting everything I had sacrificed for them. Now, I don't help people for applause or to be appreciated. Still, to be attacked by someone I'd proven my love for is a bitter betrayal. I felt abandoned and foolish. I was crushed.

During that time, I came home and found pieces of paper stuck with black electrical tape on various mirrors. Carlos and I had just remodeled our bathroom and done some sweet decorating. The strips of electrical tape did not match my chosen décor. Carlos' messages did not match my current mood, either. But that was his point.

My husband said, "Nope. I know you're hurt, and this thing has thrown you, but it's gotten enough attention now. You're going to stop what you're doing and read these notes from God. Speak these truths over yourself and declare goodness in your life. You'll forgive these people and shake it off so you can heal and move on with Jesus."

My pride wasn't quite ready to "shake it off," but I knew he was right — the longer I held onto the offense, the deeper unforgiveness would bore into my soul. *Forgive. Do it quickly.*

Reluctantly, I read those messages to myself each day. I could only whisper them at first until I felt the spirit of God's healing give a confident voice to His promises. I want you to declare those same truths over your life and your dreams.

Declare It!

1. "I declare that God believes in me and has handpicked me for a unique purpose, empowering me to dream boldly and confidently pursue those dreams."

2. "I affirm that I am strong and courageous, equipped by God to face any challenge that comes my way, knowing that He is with me every step of the journey."

3. "I proclaim that I am smart and intelligent, blessed with divine wisdom and insight, enabling me to navigate the path to my dreams and make informed decisions."

4. "I declare that I possess everything I need to transform my dreams into reality, through the strength and guidance God provides."

5. "I am confident that God has equipped me with the resilience to overcome obstacles, the tenacity to pursue my goals, and the grace to rise again after every setback."

6. "I acknowledge that I am designed to make a significant impact in this world, shining God's light and love through my actions and positively influencing the lives of others."

7. "I assert that my life is a testament to God's faithfulness, and every step I take towards my goals is guided by His hand and infused with His wisdom."

8. "I am a vessel of God's peace and creativity, bringing innovation and solutions to the world around me, making a difference through my God-given talents and abilities."

9. "I affirm that I am surrounded by God's favor and protection, which propels me forward in my journey to achieve my dreams and fulfill my destiny."

10. "I declare that with God by my side, there is no dream too big, no challenge insurmountable, and no goal unreachable. I am destined to thrive, inspire, and leave a legacy of faith and achievement."

No more letting the enemy shut your mind down, no more being defeated, no more living a life of lack, no more letting other's words and actions take you off your course with bitterness.

It's time to embrace our God-given potential with joy, courage, and a spirit of tenacity. When we dare to dream again, we're unstoppable with Christ by our side. So, let's pull each other up and leap into the ocean of possibilities together. With faith as our compass, there's no limit to how far we can go.

Resilience isn't about avoiding failure or hardship but how we respond to it. Instead of letting setbacks hold us back, we can use them as a springboard to success.

On the next pages are ways to pump yourself full of faith, hope, perseverance, and promise.

Now, let's step boldly into the dreams God has placed in our hearts. Let's mend the cracks in our belief with faith and remember our worth in Christ. Together, with Jesus as our guide, let's dream bigger, reach higher, and know that no dream is too distant. What are you afraid of? We'll take an honest look at that question in Week Five.

> It's not about how hard you hit. It's about how hard you can get hit and keep moving forward."
>
> Rocky Balboa, *Rocky*

7 Game-Changing Habits for Transformational Outcomes

Bounce Back

1. **Own Your Actions.**

   Benefit: Learn from mistakes, grow, and make better decisions in the future. By taking responsibility for your choices, you have control over your life and can build trust with others.

2. **Clarify Your Dream.**

   Benefit: Clearly defining your goal helps you align your efforts and create a roadmap to success. A vivid vision also keeps you motivated and focused.

3. **Set SMART Goals.**

   Benefit: Breaking down your dream into specific, measurable goals with deadlines allows for tracking progress, setting realistic targets, keeping you on track with your overall vision.

4. **Stay Positive.**

   Benefit: Cultivating a positive mindset enhances well-being. Focus on finding solutions instead of dwelling on problems and cultivate gratitude for what you have.

5. **Build Resilience.**

   Benefits: Embrace failure as a learning opportunity and develop coping strategies. View obstacles as stepping stones.

6. **Know Your Strengths.**

   Benefit: Identify what helps you bounce back from setbacks and leverage those strengths.

7. **Take Consistent Action.**

   Benefit: Stay committed to your goals and keep moving forward, one step at a time.

DREAM COME TRUE
Katherine Switzer

Kathrine Virginia Switzer made history in 1967 when she became the first woman to officially register for the Boston Marathon. She completed the race back then, and she just did it again!

During her first time, the Boston Marathon was a male-dominated event. To get around that, Switzer registered with her initials, K.V. Switzer, to conceal her gender. A woman in the race was not against the rules. In fact, it would have been so far outside the norm that it never crossed anyone's mind to establish an exclusionary rule — not until Kathrine. When the race manager, Jock Semple, saw her running alongside the men, he was furious.

Reporter Dawne Gee wrote, "Switzer never saw him coming. She was already in her stride but she heard the noise of his hard leather shoes on the street as he came up behind her. ' He cussed me and said get out of my race and tried to rip the numbers off,' she said in a shout. 'He got the corner of the one on my back. It was a terrible, terrible moment in my life.' It is a moment that sparked worldwide controversy and changed the face of sports."[1,2]

Switzer continues to fight and run even today, organizing more than 400 women's races in 27 countries. She was also instrumental in making the Women's Marathon an official event in the 1984 Olympic Games.

> "Sometimes the worst things in your life can become the best things in your life."
> Katherine Switzer

At 70 years old, Switzer once again donned number 261 to participate in the Boston Marathon, commemorating the 50th anniversary of her historic first official entrance and completion of the race. This time, she completed it in four hours and 20 minutes, just 24 minutes slower than her run at the age of 20.

The bib number given to K.V. Switzer, 261, has been retired and given the honor her resilience deserves. Now, the number takes on new meaning through Switzer's global non-profit for women, *261-Fearless*.

WEEK 5

Embrace Fear~~lessness~~
Conquer Doubt and Choose Courage

I was about fifteen years old on a youth missions trip the first time I went white water rafting. I was nervous, but the kind of nervousness that comes from an exhilarating experience. So when I heard about the excursion in Tennessee several years later, I was all in! The Ocoee River is where the Olympics were held in 1996. They have different sections of the course to accommodate any skill level. Class I is more of a lazy river experience, up to Level VI, which is "rarely run, dangerous and hazardous to life." I signed up for a four-person Class V: "expert; complex and demanding, large drops." I am naturally competitive, so after one successful rafting trip five years prior, I thought I was an Olympian.

I probably should've reconsidered when I found out special insurance was required, plus about ten pages of liability waivers to sign. The forms were just one requirement shy of a Do Not Resuscitate order and Organ Donation information. Carlos and I were dating then; all he could do was laugh and shake his head at me. I thought I was tough stuff, but part of my motivation may have been to show off for this cute guy. Show no fear! Really, though, *What could go wrong?*

Within ten minutes on the water, I was thrown out of the raft three times.

It sounds funny now, but it was really scary. Ten tons of water rushed on all sides, rolling me beneath one of the other rafts. I was trapped, struggling to escape from underneath the vessel, but the rapids fought against me. When I finally got free, the water slammed me against a rock just before they pulled me into the raft. Gasping and coughing, I lay there limp and bleeding, grateful to be alive with no more than a busted elbow and bruised ego. I still have the scar to prove it.

Not all scars are physical or visible, but many of us have residual injuries from trying to take on too much, making unwise or unhealthy choices, or experiencing an unsuccessful run at a new adventure. We want to quit. But, quitting is not always a viable or valuable option.

Out of danger but still shaken and exhausted, I wanted my white water escapade to end. *Stop the ride. I want off!* But there was no pulling over to the side. For me, there was still an hour on the psychopathic water before we got to the bend where we could take a break.

Some journeys are like that. Once you make the commitment, you're in it. There's no going back, no stopping mid-way. You have to ride it out through the vicious waters and jagged rocks to a place of peace and safety. There is no time to panic, cry, or throw a fit; all your strength and focus is on making it to the other side. The real challenge to our courage comes when quitting *is* an option.

I didn't have a choice but to keep going. What if, after my near-drowning, I'd had the option to be divinely transported right up out of that entire scene? Would I have spared myself the effort of being brave? I felt fearless after that whitewater experience, but my courage wasn't proven in the first leg of the trip before the first break. You see, real courage is proven when we're terrified but keep going anyway — when we *could* bow out but don't.

After the lunch break, I got my gear and got back in the raft. It had been a harrowing first-leg, but I knew if I bailed, that experience could have defined how I viewed every new adventure or unfamiliar opportunity. I wasn't going out like that.

Fear encourages us to play it safe and avoid risks. We become afraid of taking chances because they could lead to disappointment or failure. However, pursuing our dreams often involves stepping into the unknown and taking calculated risks. Do not let fear trap you in your comfort zone and prevent you from growing and progressing.

When you are tempted to cling to the familiar at the expense of the future, take decisive action in the direction of your goal. One decision in support of your vision will motivate you on to the rest. After my mishap on the water, we stopped for a lunch break. I mustered the courage to go back out on the water. The first action toward that end was to put my gear back on. Ten minutes later, I grabbed my paddle and began walking in the direction of the water. Then I got in the raft. When the other three were in, we pushed off. With each action, I set myself up to achieve my objective. When you have the option of playing it safe in mediocrity, choose instead to make one intentional step toward pursuing something extraordinary. Do not abandon your purpose!

> **Real courage is proven when we're terrified but keep going anyway.**

Sometimes, all it takes to rob fear of it's influence is to view it through a different lense. I could view falling out of the boat as a failure and leave it at, "I'm just not cut out for this." Or I can focus on the rescue and trust that, "Sink or swim, God has me in His hand." We each have an option to stop our course at failure or fear, or fear of failure. We can also choose to take a beat, get back in it, and create an Against All Odds victory story instead.

You can redefine a moment and dictate how it affects you. Don't let discouragement or doubt decide your future. Tell your anxiety what it will to mean to your next decision. Fear doesn't mean helplessness. Go ahead and feel afraid — do the thing anyway. That's what courage is.

Maybe you're thinking, *Sure, Rosalinda, but your near-drowning was an act of nature. I'm drowning in the natural consequences of my bad choices and weaknesses.*

The cause of our terrifying situation is something to give some attention to. Suppose your choices have put you in a fearful situation. In that case, you can still course-correct through confession and obedience from now on. There may still be fall-out from your mistakes, but God will bless your humility and repentance. Remember Jonah?

Jonah, a Hebrew prophet, received a divine instruction from God. He was tasked with preaching against the evil in Nineveh, an influential city considered an enemy of Israel. However, Jonah was afraid of this mission. The city's notorious reputation and the potential danger it posed led him to flee from God's command. Instead of going to Nineveh, he boarded a ship destined for Tarshish, heading in the opposite direction (Jonah 1:1-3).

God stirred up a fierce storm during the sea voyage, putting everyone on board in danger. The superstitious crew began praying to their own gods because they knew Jonah must have gotten on the bad side of one of them. The captain questioned Jonah, asking him who which god he served. Jonah said, "I am a Hebrew and I worship the Lord, the God of heaven, who made the sea and the dry land" (Jonah 1:4-9).

If you have ever made a poor decision that has affected others negatively, you can feel the world's weight is resting on your shoulders. The guilt can be suffocating, consuming your thoughts and leaving you feeling isolated in your remorse. Every time you close your eyes, you may see the faces of those you have hurt, haunted by their disappointment and pain. It becomes a burden that you carry with you every waking moment, a heavy anchor dragging you down into a sea of regret. Will you have the courage to make it right and salvage those relationships?

Jonah regretted the position he'd put these men in and told them to throw him overboard. They tried to find another solution, but had to let him go to save their own lives.

I know this story does not sound very positive so far, but I want you to notice a couple of encouraging things before we go on:

If you make a mistake, you don't have to keep making them. Choose the courage to operate with integrity, humility, and selflessness going forward. When Jonah saw what his decision was doing to other people, he tried to make it right. He confessed and tried to fix the catastrophe he had caused.

God will even use your wrongs to get others right with Him. When the crew threw Jonah overboard, the sea immediately became calm and quiet. These men on the boat worshipped false gods. But when they saw God's power and His compassion in sparing their lives, they turned to Him and offered a sacrifice to the Lord (Jonah 1:15-16).

God will always operate in our best interest. Sometimes, God rescues us immediately. Other times, He leaves us stewing with whatever the whale ate for breakfast. Whatever is best for us is what the Lord will design. That, you can count on.

If you are battling fear because of the result of a poor choice you've made, be encouraged: you can make a better choice! Just know there may be residual consequences between repentance and restoration.

I'd Like to Change My Answer, Please!

While the guys on the boat were offering sacrifices to the Lord, the Lord was offering Jonah to a whale. Jonah prayed to the Lord for three days and nights and got back in line with His purpose. Then, at God's command, the fish spit him onto the shore (Jonah 2).

Jonah picked up the original mission and traveled to Nineveh to deliver God's warning. To everyone's amazement, the people of Nineveh heeded Jonah's words and repented. They fasted and turned away from their sinful behaviors, and God spared them (Jonah 3).

Jonah's story isn't like anyone else's, but the cause of his misadventure is very relatable to most of us.

Fear.

1. Confront Fear Head-On

"For God gave us a spirit not of fear but of power and love and self-control." - 2 Timothy 1:7

Fear is not from God but rather a hindrance to embracing our dreams fully. By tapping into the power, love, and self-control granted to us, we can courageously confront fear and confidently pursue our dreams.

2. Persist Through Adversity

"Consider it pure joy, my brothers and sisters, whenever you face trials of many kinds because you know that the testing of your faith produces perseverance." - James 1:2-3

Just as trials produce perseverance, overcoming challenges on the path to our dreams strengthens our resolve and fortifies our journey towards fulfillment.

3. Trust in Divine Timing and Guidance

"Trust in the Lord with all your heart and lean not on your own understanding; in all your ways submit to him, and he will make your paths straight." - Proverbs 3:5-6

By submitting our plans and dreams to God, we open ourselves to His divine direction, knowing He will lead us on the straight path toward our desired destinations.

The longer Jonah allowed fear to control him, the more it chipped away at his self-confidence. Is that where you are? Has fear gradually eroded your belief in your ability to carry out God's mission? It is time to push harder, stay focused, confront doubts, embrace courage, and unlock the power within you to overcome any obstacle that stands in the way of your dreams. Maybe it's a new career path, a challenging goal, or a dream you've held onto for years. Perhaps a brand new opportunity is facing you, but it comes with challenging opposition. It may be disguised as a Philistine. A really big one.

The well-known account of David and Goliath tells the tale of a young shepherd boy who bravely faced off against a giant Philistine warrior named Goliath. Despite being the youngest of his brothers, David was filled with courage and faith as he approached Goliath on the battlefield. Unlike the other Israelites, who were afraid to confront Goliath, David refused to wear any armor. Instead, he relied on his trusty sling and five smooth stones.

> "David said to the Philistine, 'You come against me with sword and spear and javelin, but I come against you in the name of the Lord Almighty, the God of the armies of Israel, whom you have defied. This day the Lord will deliver you into my hands, and I'll strike you down and cut off your head. This very day I will give the carcasses of the Philistine army to the birds and the wild animals, and the whole world will know that there is a God in Israel. All those gathered here will know that it is not by sword or spear that the Lord saves; for the battle is the Lord's, and he will give all of you into our hands.'"
>
> — 1 Samuel 17:42-47 (NIV)

In the name of the Lord Almighty, David slung a stone at Goliath's head, knocking him down. Then, he used Goliath's own sword to kill him and cut off his head as a symbol of victory over their enemies.

🚀 Jonah ran. **David stepped up.**

🚀 Jonah was impulsive. **David was resilient.**

🚀 Jonah doubted. **David delivered.**

In moments when you're tempted to respond more like Jonah than David, allowing fear to make you forget who you are, remember what David said to Saul when he volunteered to face Goliath.

> "Your servant has been keeping his father's sheep. When a lion or a bear came and carried off a sheep from the flock, I went after it, struck it and rescued the sheep from its mouth. When it turned on me, I seized it by its hair, struck it and killed it. Your servant has killed both the lion and the bear; this uncircumcised Philistine will be like one of them, because he has defied the armies of the living God. The Lord who rescued me from the paw of the lion and the paw of the bear will rescue me from the hand of this Philistine."
>
> — 1 Samuel 17:34-37 (NIV)

The greatest weapon against fear and anxiety is remembering how the Lord has brought you through in the past and recognizing that He has given you everything you need to come through victorious.

He did it before. He'll do it again.

What fears or obstacles are you facing today that require a leap of faith and courage? How can you draw strength from David's example and trust God's provision as you confront your giants?

As we reflect on David's story and the principles of courage and faith it embodies, we can turn to prayer as a powerful tool for growth and application in our lives.

Search your heart in prayer, inviting God to reveal any areas where fear may be holding you back. Ask Him to illuminate doubts and insecurities, and to show you where you need His strength and guidance to overcome obstacles.

Pray for courage and faith to step out in obedience, just as David did when he faced Goliath. Ask God to fill you with His Spirit and empower you to take bold steps toward your dreams, trusting in His provision and protection every step of the way.

Reflect on lessons from David's story—the importance of trusting God, facing your fears head-on, and stepping out in faith. Ask God to help apply these principles in your life and to give you the wisdom and discernment to recognize opportunities for growth and courage.

Commit to walking in obedience to God's leading, even when challenging or uncomfortable. Ask Him to strengthen your resolve and deepen your faith as you strive to live fearlessly and pursue the dreams He has placed in your heart.

> *"Have I not commanded you? Be strong and courageous. Do not be afraid; do not be discouraged, for the Lord your God will be with you wherever you go."*
>
> — Joshua 1:9 (NIV)

With God by your side, you can confidently face your fears, knowing you are never alone.

> **"You'll have bad times, but it'll always wake you up to the good stuff you weren't paying attention to."**
>
> — Sean, *Good Will Hunting*

7 Game-Changing Habits for Transformational Outcomes

Fear Not

1. **Identify Your Fears.**

   Benefit: Break down fear into its specific components (Fear of rejection, failure, disappointing others) Understanding the underlying elements helps you address them more effectively.

2. **Neutralize the Fear Component.**

   Benefit: Confronting and replacing negative, outdated, or incorrect messages makes room for empowering thoughts.

3. **Challenge Limiting Beliefs.**

   Benefit: Replacing distorted beliefs with empowering ones help you see failures as opportunities for growth and believe in our ability to learn and improve.

4. Take Small Steps.

Benefit: Gradually stepping outside your comfort zone builds resilience and confidence. Recognize that personal growth is a journey and setbacks are a natural part of it.

5. Learn to Trust Yourself.

Benefit: By researching and learning what you need, you can minimize fear. Even if you make a mistake, you can correct it.

6. Imagine a Positive Outcome.

Benefit: Using your imagination to envision positive scenarios. consciously shift your focus to a successful outcome, weakening your fear response.

7. Seek Support.

Benefit: Sharing dreams with trusted friends, mentors, or coaches who can offer encouragement, advice, and accountability.

DREAM COME TRUE

Kendra Scott

In 2002, just three months after becoming a mother, Kendra Scott founded her own jewelry company with only $500 as an initial investment.

Her first business, *Hat Box* in Austin, was not successful, but that didn't stop her from pursuing her dreams. Kendra took a risk by creating her own brand. It wasn't an easy journey, as she recalls battling a fear of rejection when her line wasn't immediately accepted. But instead of giving up, she found the courage to try again at a different store and persevered.

Now, Kendra Scott Jewelry is a global brand appealing to a wide audience, including sorority girls, moms, and even celebrities like Taylor Swift. Her company grew from a small startup in her spare bedroom to a billion-dollar brand by 2016. Despite being a successful entrepreneur, Scott is also known for her philanthropic work and support for causes like breast cancer research. She even established the Kendra Scott Women's Entrepreneurial Leadership Institute in partnership with The University of Texas at Austin to empower future female leaders. In addition to appearing as the only female guest "shark" on Season 12 of *Shark Tank*, Scott continues to make an impact as the executive chairman, chief creative officer, and majority owner of her company.

> "As women, we feel like [it's] a sign of weakness if we ask for help and to me, it is the greatest sign of strength."
>
> Kendra Scott

Recently, she released a memoir titled "Born to Shine: Do Good, Find Your Joy, and Build a Life You Love," where she shares the rewards, challenges, and lessons learned from her journey. Looking back on those early days, Scott emphasizes the importance of seeking help when needed. Kendra Scott's story exemplifies the power of persistence, innovation, and a commitment to making a positive impact.

WEEK 6

Reach Beyond the Sky
Developing Infinite Potential

When I was a child, the kids always had something up and running in my neighborhood. We were designing and building forts, packing snacks and flashlights for some secret adventure (usually in a friend's backyard), or attempting to solve the mystery of time travel. Written in crayon and marker on the thick, tan paper of grocery bags were the formulas for many a multi-million dollar business venture. It never occurred to any of us to try to do it alone. What fun would that be?

This week, we're shifting our focus to standing in confidence on the backs of the proven faith of others. Help and encouragement from those who know you best can make all the difference in your journey to success. As you navigate the ups and downs of life, receiving motivation and guidance is what you need to keep moving forward. Whether it's family members, friends, mentors, or colleagues, surrounding yourself with positive influences can help you stay motivated and focused. No one achieves greatness alone – we all need a little help along the way. As Kendra Scott pointed out, asking for help is the greatest sign of strength. Cultivate meaningful connections and lean on your network—it's essential for your success!

Moses, a prominent character in the Old Testament, took heed of his father-in-law Jethro's guidance. Jethro suggested that Moses delegate tasks by appointing capable leaders to assist him in governing and judging the Israelite people. Moses followed this advice, which not only improved leadership efficiency but also prevented exhaustion and burnout. In doing so, Moses displayed humility and wisdom, acknowledging that successful leadership requires collaboration and delegation.

Moses followed God's plan but also understood the importance of adapting the particulars when necessary. When Jethro offered advice, Moses had the wisdom to listen and alter his leadership style. By delegating responsibilities, the weight was lifted for all involved.

Just as Moses had his loyal advisors by his side during his most challenging moments, we also need a team of supportive allies to encourage, uplift, and journey alongside us as we believe in the promises and dreams God has placed in our hearts.

Take a moment to reflect on the people in your life who have stood by you through thick and thin. Who cheers you on, believes in your potential, and offers a shoulder to lean on when times get tough? These individuals make up your Dream Team—the ones who will celebrate your victories, pull you up when you stumble, and not be afraid to give you a good kick in the rut when you need to get moving.

As you compile your Dream Team, remember that each member plays a unique and valuable role in supporting and encouraging you along your journey. Lean on them, seek their wisdom and guidance, and celebrate the victories and milestones together.

Now, let's create a list of those who can offer emotional and spiritual support as we embark on this journey of faith and fulfillment.

Consider reaching out to:

Family members who have always been there for you, providing love, encouragement, and unwavering support.

Close friends who understand your dreams and aspirations and cheer you on every step of the way.

Mentors or spiritual advisors who can offer guidance, wisdom, and prayer support as you navigate the ups and downs of pursuing your dreams.

Fellow believers who share your faith and values and can provide spiritual encouragement and accountability.

Support groups or community organizations where you can connect with like-minded individuals who are also pursuing their dreams and goals.

I want to address a concern that some of us may face: the feeling of not having a strong support system to lean on. If you are more of the lone-wolf type or feel isolated, you do not have to stay that way. Even if you don't currently have people on your list, there is hope and reinforcement to be found as you dream big and strive to accomplish great things.

You are not alone. No matter how we may feel at times, none of us is ever alone. You are not going it on your own. God is with you every step of the way, guiding and directing your path. He sees the desires of your heart and knows the dreams you long to pursue. Trust in His promises and lean on His strength as you step out in faith.

Seek opportunities to connect. Look for others who share your passions and aspirations. This could involve joining online communities, attending networking events, or volunteering with organizations aligned with your interests. By putting yourself out there and engaging with like-minded individuals, you may find a kindred spirit who can offer support and encouragement along the way.

Cultivate relationships. Look for individuals who have walked a similar path or possess qualities and experiences you admire. Mentors or advisors can offer guidance, wisdom, and prayer support. Their insights and perspectives can be invaluable as you navigate the challenges and opportunities of pursuing your dreams.

Remember that God is your source. Your strength, wisdom, and provision come from the Lord. Trust in His timing and plan for your life, knowing He is working all things together for your good. Even if the road ahead seems uncertain or lonely at times, rest in the assurance that God is faithful to fulfill the dreams He has placed in your heart.

Surround yourself with supportive allies who will walk alongside you. With your team backing you, no obstacle can stand. You will achieve the extraordinary things that God has destined for you.

How big can you dream? What ideas can you come up with? What keeps you up at night? What do you hear or see that lights up a spark in your soul? You may have outgrown some of your childhood ambitions, but hold on to your childlike faith and don't try to do it without a great crew (Especially if time travel is being considered).

How Big Are Your Dreams?

My mother loved musicals. We grew up watching Judy Garland in *The Wizard of Oz*, plus *The Sound of Music*, *My Fair Lady*, *Oklahoma*, and *The Music Man*. If you're familiar with my dad's past, you know I saw West Side Story more than a dozen times. Every story, every song would sweep me away in my imagination. I placed myself in the scenes and was carried to another dimension where anything could happen.

I knew even back then that impossibilities are the best abilities.

My dad would pause the movies in the middle and announce, "It's time for our Intermission Show!" All four of us kids would do a little song and dance or perform some skit we came up with in the hallway minutes before. Still, it wasn't just childish play to me. In my heart, it struck something deeper. When I grow up, I want to do this forever, I thought.

Imagination is a powerful thing. I wanted to ride that red trolly on *Mr. Roger's Neighborhood* and have a little chat with Lady Aberlin and Daniel Tiger. Dreams were encouraged. I knew even back then that impossibilities are the best abilities . Back then, we believed we could be anything we wanted to be. I wanted to be one of Lawrence Welk's dancers.

I wasn't even born when "The Lawrence Welk Show" emerged in the early '50s. We would watch the reruns, and I was in awe of the sophisticated women with their beautiful, flowing ball gowns swooshing across the floor with a handsome tuxedoed man. Their smiles, music, and dance numbers were elegant, and I dreamed of being one of them. I pictured myself gliding across the dance floor with the bubbles around me and Welk clapping and saying, "Wunnerful! Wunnerful!" There was nothing more I wanted to do than to sing and dance and be on Broadway.

I joined every choir I could, entered contests and recitals, and was thrilled to travel to Florida to compete with my high school's show choir from Virginia. Our selection was a hat and cane song and dance. I felt like Debbie Reynolds with Gene Kelly in *Dancing in the Rain*. My family and my friends were always so encouraging. Although I never made it to the lights of Broadway, I am grateful to have been surrounded by people who let me dream larger than life. The freedom to dream has built an entrepreneurial spirit within me, a sense of wonder, and a gumption to stick to it. Not all of my endeavors have panned out; but the dreams that have come true would have never gotten off the ground if I'd stopped believing they could.

I encourage you to return to that childlike mindset of curiosity and possibilities — before the disappointments and responsibilities diminished your nature to dream. Children are like little dream machines, firing off wild ideas faster than kernels exploding in a movie popcorn machine. Their minds are like open playgrounds, free from the chains of "can't" and "won't," where unicorns roam freely, and rocket ships take voyages to distant galaxies. So many places to travel with imagination, and not much else.

We didn't have the money to shop at *Toys R Us*. We had duct tape and boxes. My brother and sisters and I took whatever we could get our hands on around the house and became the ultimate adventurers, exploring the vast landscapes of our imagination. From princesses to pirates, astronauts to superheroes, kids don't just dream it; they live it! And why not? They make up the rules as they go along, fueled by seemingly endless wonder and mischief. But then, somewhere along the line, and way too early in life, we are all handed a playbook outlining *reasonable* expectations and *rational* chances. And there they are:

Grown-up thoughts.

Reasonable and rational are the killers of revolutionary possibilities. I suppose it's to be expected. Adulthood comes crashing in like a wrecking ball, bringing bills, deadlines, and a laundry list of responsibilities — including laundry — longer than a giraffe's neck! And to think, I *wanted* that day to come!

Parents tell kids to "enjoy childhood while you still can." I thought the advice was some sort of parental trickery until my first car insurance premium came due. Gas, food, and cell phone expenses weren't a thing when I owned my first cardboard house and drove a Big Wheel. The dreams that once danced in technicolor now seem to fade into the background, overshadowed by the harsh glare of reality. Still, there is something more devastating than the transition from dream-filled adolescent to duty-driven adult — accepting it.

I believe for most of us, it doesn't happen all at once. For some, there is a life-altering event that thrusts someone into adult responsibilities prematurely, but at some point for most, the "shoulds" and "musts" chase away the whimsical adventures of childhood, replacing them with the daily grind of grown-up life.

Imagine life as a magnificent carousel. In our youth, we eagerly jump onto our favorite horses and reach for the brass ring of our dreams. The horses are real. The chase is on, and the prize is ours to win! As we age, the carousel slows down, and reality sets in. We trade in our fanciful steeds for more practical workhorses and learn to navigate the mundane tasks of adulthood. The magic of the carousel fades, and the hum of responsibility takes its place. Yet, even as adults, we can catch glimpses of the old carousel and remember its wonder. The Bible encourages us to.

> "And he said: 'Truly I tell you, unless you change and become like little children, you will never enter the kingdom of heaven. Therefore, whoever takes the lowly position of this child is the greatest in the kingdom of heaven.'"
>
> — Matthew 18:3-4 (NIV)

Jesus teaches the importance of humility, trust, and innocence. He wanted to point out that these qualities are essential for a relationship with God and to experience the promise of the fullness of His kingdom.

> "Truly I tell you, anyone who will not receive the kingdom of God like a little child will never enter it."
>
> — Mark 10:15 (NIV)

Simplicity, trust, and dependence define childlike faith. As grown-ups, we must also put our trust in God with a similar level of innocence and reliance. Now I want you to engage in a symbolic exercise to show your dependence on the Lord. Get a piece of paper and write down your dream. Hold it in your hands for a moment. Now, stretch it out towards God and say this prayer—

Heavenly Father, As I come before You today, I humbly surrender my dreams into Your loving hands. With childlike faith, I trust that You see the desires of my heart and know the path ahead. I release any fears or doubts that may hold me back and place my complete trust in Your divine provision. Lord, You know the dreams and aspirations that stir within me, and I offer them up to You, knowing that Your plans for me far exceed anything I could imagine. Give me the courage to let go of my plans and embrace Your perfect will for my life.

Help me walk in faith, even when the path seems uncertain.

I believe, Lord, that You are the ultimate provider, and I trust in Your promise to equip me with everything I need to fulfill the purpose You have for me. Open doors that no one can shut and guide me along the path You have prepared for me. Give me wisdom to discern Your will and strength to follow it wholeheartedly. Thank You, Father, for Your faithfulness and Your unending love. I surrender my dreams to You, knowing that You will work all things together for my good. May Your will be done in my life, and may Your name be glorified through every step I take. In Jesus' name, I pray, Amen.

Thank you for praying that prayer with me. Each morning, take time to approach God with the same wide-eyed wonder and unwavering trust of a child. God is your loving Father who cares deeply for you, His child. Get ready; this is your season!

Let's dust off those old dreams, shake off the cobwebs, and dive headfirst into the sea of possibility once again! Let's reclaim that childlike wonder and embrace the magic of imagination. Who says grown-ups can't have fun, too? After all, the world is our playground, and the only limit to what we can achieve is the boundary of our own imagination. So, what do you say? Ready to dream big and live even bigger? Let's do this!

Design Your Launch Plan

Fuel the Vision

Just like a rocket needs fuel to launch, our dreams require a clear vision. Take time to visualize your dream in vivid detail. What does success look like? How will it feel when you achieve it?

One of my favorite phone screen backgrounds is my Vision Board. It brings me joy to glance at it and see how many milestones I've achieved, but it also serves as a gentle nudge for the areas I still need to focus on. Creating a Vision Board for your dream is as simple as gathering images, quotes, and words that resonate with your aspirations and then compiling them into a collage. This visual representation acts as a daily reminder of your goals and dreams, so place it somewhere prominent where you'll encounter it often, such as your desk or bedroom wall.

When I decided to write my first book, "Dare to Begin Again," I penned a date on a yellow sticky note and stuck it on the wall beside my bed. Every morning, that date greeted me, a tangible reminder of the challenge I had set for myself. Though I didn't quite meet that deadline, it served as fuel, propelling me into action and guiding me through the necessary steps to complete the project just a few months later.

Build the Launch Pad

Venice Skinner is a great friend of mine who goes to my church, *New Life Outreach*, in Richmond, Virginia. Venice is an artist who works with oil and also makes ceramics. She is a favorite vendor among the women who attend my Bella Conference each year. One day, she gave me a beautiful gift for my desk. My friend presented me with a set of ceramic coasters, each featuring a stunning African-American woman from her original artwork. These individual works of art came from her imagination and through her hands. They really are breathtaking.

Every successful launch requires a solid foundation. Venice has a natural talent but knows that talent alone can only take you so far. She has spent years honing her skills, working with various techniques and mediums, admiring the work of others, and gleaning insight and inspiration from other styles.

Building your launch pad begins with identifying your resources, from skills to support systems, and crafting a strategic plan of action. Take inventory of your strengths and areas for growth, research your field, and establish a supportive network to guide you. Develop a clear roadmap with actionable steps, set deadlines, and remember to prioritize self-care. Seek feedback, stay flexible, and adapt to navigate challenges and seize opportunities. With a strong foundation and a flexible approach, you'll be ready to ignite your dreams and soar to new heights.

When taking on a new venture, it's vital that you have researched and checked your demographics and competition, as well as assessed previous wins and losses. Include the counsel of others for motivation and advice; most of all, seek the Lord's guidance in prayer.

Ignite Passion

Just as a rocket's engines ignite with intense heat, our dreams need passion to propel them forward. Reignite your enthusiasm for your dream by reminding yourself why it matters to you and the impact it could have on others.

If you are alone in this stage of your dream adventure, let me turn you on to an old Gospel song that's come in handy in my life more than once. When there was noone around to cheer me on, or I was in a situation others could not relate to, I sang these words from Donald Lawrence's "Encourage Yourself"[13] to myself:

> *Sometimes you have to encourage yourself*
> *Sometimes you have to speak victory during the test*
> *And no matter how you feel*
> *Speak the word, and you will be healed*
> *Speak over yourself*
> *Encourage yourself in the Lord*

> *Sometimes you (sometimes you) have to encourage yourself*
> *Gotta pat your own self on the back, yeah, yeah*
> *Sometimes you have to speak victory during the test*
> *And no matter how you feel (no matter how you feel)*
> *Speak the word over your life, oh, oh*
> *Speak the word, and you will be healed (you will be healed)*
> *Speak over yourself (speak over yourself)*
> *Encourage yourself (encourage yourself) in the Lord*

Navigate Obstacles

Every journey has challenges, and launching into the unknown can be daunting. Anticipate potential obstacles and develop strategies for overcoming them. Remember, setbacks are growth opportunities.

Back in high school, I gave track a shot. Now, let me tell you, I wasn't exactly built for sprinting, but one day, our coach decided it was hurdle time. I remember thinking, *Well, this will be the end of me.* I was ready to throw in the towel before I even started, but Coach addressed the fear in my eyes.

Instead of letting me give up, he showed me a strategy to tackle those hurdles — the ones on the track and those in my mind. Before I knew it, I was leaping over them like a pro. His guidance was a game-changer. Like in track, you'll face hurdles on your journey to success. But once you spot them, you can start working out how to overcome them. With the right strategy and a bit of determination, those obstacles won't stand a chance.

Check Systems

Before lift-off, it's essential to ensure all systems are GO. Take time to evaluate your plan, identifying any weak points or areas that need improvement. Adjust your course as necessary to maximize your chances of success.

Can you imagine strapping yourself into a rocket ship headed for space without a systems check? That would be downright bonkers, right? Who in their right mind would take off without making sure everything's in tip-top shape? It's like driving a car without checking the gas gauge or the tires — just asking for trouble!

No Troubles! Stay away from trouble.

So, before we even think about launching into our own big adventures, let's take a cue from those savvy astronauts and do some system checks of our own. Think of it as our way of making sure all thrusters are firing before we embark on our journey. After all, we want to ensure we're ready for whatever may happen, don't we? So, let's roll up our sleeves, dig into the details, and make sure we're good to go before we take that leap into the great unknown!

Count Down

As launch day approaches, excitement builds, but so does nervousness. Stay focused on your goal, taking one step at a time. Break down your plan into manageable tasks and celebrate each milestone.

What is your plan? Take a moment and fill in the blanks.

As launch day approaches, I'm feeling a mix of excitement and nervousness. But I'm staying focused _____ on my goal of. My plan is to take it one step at a time. I'll start by breaking down my overall goal into smaller, manageable tasks. For example, my first milestone is _____

To achieve this, I'll need to _____.

Once I reach this milestone, I'll celebrate by _____

Then, I'll move on to the next step, which is _____

I'll continue this process until I've reached my ultimate goal of

_____. I'll stay flexible and open to adjustments as needed along the way. With each milestone I achieve, I'll take a moment to acknowledge my progress and celebrate how far I've come.

Lift-off

Finally, the moment arrives to ignite the engines and soar into the sky. Embrace the exhilaration of seeing your dreams take flight, trusting in the groundwork you've laid and the vision that propels you forward. Remember, this is just the beginning of an incredible journey.

In Week 5, we compared David and Jonah's different initial responses to the assignments of the Lord, and we learned a lot from David.

The many times I've heard the story of David and Goliath, it's been told that the young shepherd ousted the Philistine with nothing but a slingshot. We say the odds were against David. But were they? David was backed by the Almighty God. You don't get better odds than that. You are standing before your giants with the same assurance — this thing is rigged in your favor, just like it was for David.

David knew his future wasn't about only personal success; yours isn't for you, either. Your goal is meant to fulfill God's purposes on the earth for His Kingdom. But that doesn't mean the task will be easy.

David's journey to kingship was fraught with challenges and obstacles, including persecution from King Saul, betrayal from his family, and internal strife within his kingdom. However, David remained faithful to God and relied on Him for guidance and strength. Do not forget your Source.

Despite his flaws and mistakes, David's reign as king was marked by moments of triumph, prosperity, and God's favor. His story teaches us the importance of faith, resilience, and perseverance in pursuing our dreams, even in the face of adversity. With God's help, ordinary individuals can accomplish extraordinary things and fulfill their God-given destiny. That means you, friend.

A few weeks back, I told you I had a stint as a cheerleader. Now, I will swallow my pride and share that story.

The idea of pom poms and kicks may be hard to reconcile with the white water rafting, hurdle jumping, fort-builder you've been getting to know, so brace yourself. I was indeed more into any sport involving running, jumping, and occasionally shoving. I was not dainty, hence the unrealized dream of becoming a ballerina on Broadway. Naturally, in my mind, the next best thing was kicking, jumping, and screaming while others yelled and did flips all around me. So, I would become a cheerleader. Tryouts were Saturday morning.

I began to visualize myself in that cute little outfit, getting all the boys' attention, tossing pom poms, chanting, dancing, and cheering the crowd on. A requirement they never mentioned was doing a cartwheel into a split. A cartwheel. Into. A. Split.

I could do a cartwheel but had never done the splits. I mean, not on purpose. The one time I did accomplish the splits, black ice was involved. I knew that wasn't the case, but I was determined not to sneak out. The announcer squeaked my name over the loudspeaker, "Rosalinda, you're next." I did the cheer and ramped up for the grand finale.

With the spirit of Gold Medalist Mary Lou Retton, I threw my body up in the air and —

SNAP!

I did not stick the landing.

The judges jumped up in horror. The gym went silent. And me? Not willing to concede, I threw my hand into the air like a superstar gymnast who had not just tried to break herself in half. I didn't quite do the splits, but nothing was broken, and I made the squad! I was an official cheerleader.

You are going to make it, and you can do more than you think you can. You are stronger than you think, and God makes all things possible. Just like David trusted in God's strength and defeated Goliath, you will also conquer your obstacles.

You are ready for Lift-off!

> Something's comin', something good, if I can wait.
>
> — West Side Story

7 Game-Changing Habits for Transformational Outcomes

Develop Potential

1. Define Your Goals.

   Benefit: Implement productivity hacks to streamline your workflow and maximize efficiency.

2. Focus Techniques.

   Benefit: Practice focus techniques and prayer to minimize distractions.

3. Delegate Wisely.

   Benefit: Delegate tasks that don't align with your strengths to free up time for high-value activities.

4. **Energy Management.**

   Benefit: Manage your energy levels by prioritizing sleep, nutrition, and exercise.

5. **Technology Optimization.**

   Benefit: Use technology to your advantage by leveraging tools and apps that boost productivity.

6. **Batching Tasks.**

   Benefit: Group similar tasks together and tackle them in batches to minimize context switching.

7. **Review and Reflect.**

   Benefit: Regularly review your progress and reflect on what's working and what can be improved.

DREAM COME TRUE

The Mardini Sisters

The Mardini sisters, Yusra and Sara, were rising stars in the world of professional swimming in Syria, trained by their father who was also a former national swimmer. However, their lives were disrupted when the Syrian Revolution and civil war began. In 2015, they made the difficult decision to flee their home country with their cousin Nizar, seeking refuge in Europe. Their journey was fraught with difficulties as they faced social stigma and unscrupulous smugglers.

Eventually, they arrived in Turkey and planned to reach Germany by boat through Greece. But when their overcrowded dinghy's motor stalled in the Aegean Sea, Yusra, Sara, and two other passengers jumped into the water to save everyone's lives. This incredible act of courage showcased their resilience and determination. Yusra represented the Refugee Olympic Team at the 2016 Rio Olympics and the recently concluded 2020 Tokyo Olympics. Despite facing numerous challenges, she never gave up on her dream of competing on the Olympic stage.

> "We were taught how to be winners, to lead, to come up with ideas out of nowhere."
>
> Yusra Mardini

The Mardini sisters' extraordinary story has been depicted in the film "The Swimmers" directed by Sally El Hosaini, which beautifully captures their bravery and highlights the larger refugee crisis. Their inspiring tale is a poignant reminder of human strength and hope in even the most trying circumstances.

WEEK 7

Implementation
Turning Dreams into Reality

Congratulations on daring to dream again! Now that you've identified your dreams and aspirations, it's time to take concrete steps toward turning them into reality.

Week 7 is about creating a plan of action to bring your dreams to life. In the Bible, the number *seven* is often associated with completeness, perfection, and divine fulfillment. It appears frequently throughout scripture, symbolizing God's work and presence in the world — from creation in Genesis to the seven churches represented in Revelation. The number seven carries a sense of divine perfection and completion in biblical symbolism, representing God's sovereignty, authority, and fulfillment of His promises.

Implementing your dreams is like preparing for a grand adventure. Just imagine you've spent months meticulously planning a cross-country road trip. You've mapped out your route, packed your bags, and fueled up the car. As you sit behind the wheel, the engine humming with anticipation, you're about to embark on a journey filled with unknowns, breathtaking sights, and unexpected encounters.

I'll never forget the trip my husband and I took all over Europe, Russia, Dubrovnik, and Italy. We had heard amazing things about the Kremlin and were so excited to tour it. When we entered Russia, we lost our phone service. Thankfully, I had printed directions in my backpack just in case. Without it, we would have wasted time trying to get from the airport to Red Square. We cannot read the language or communicate with the people, but we had a contingency plan to make our ten-hour layover in Moscow smooth and very enjoyable. We did our little tour, had an excellent lunch, some shopping, and returned to our seats to fly off to the next destination without a hitch. We had a plan. And then we made a backup plan.

As you prepare to implement your dreams, you're standing at the threshold of a thrilling adventure. Don't let the excitement cause you to be careless in the planning. I've always said, "You can do it right, or you can do it right now." Take precautions in the prep phase, and the implementation will result in fewer mishaps. Each step you take is a milestone on your journey toward realizing your aspirations, and each fork in the road is a decision to be made toward your destination or in pursuit of distraction.

If you've traveled I-95 from Virginia to Georgia, especially between the mid-'60s to '80s you were keeping your eye out for a slew of funny billboards advertising a truck stop, souvenir shop, fireworks sales, and motel. I bet you know what I'm talking about — *South of the Border*. Dad would announce, "Here come the signs!" and we would all press our faces to the windows to read the countdown to the border between North and South Carolina. We were getting closer with every billboard: *You never sausage a place! Only 60 miles!* Then 45 miles, and 21 miles, and *You're always a weiner at Pedros! 3 miles and you're here!* Every sign increased our excitement and anticipation for tamales and sombrero-shaped, well, everything. *South of the Border* has served as a road-trip milestone from Philadelphia to Daytona Beach since before I was born. Look up. Don't miss your milestone signs on your journey. They stand as proof that you're on the right road, making progress, and should celebrate all you have achieved so far. Read the signs. You are on your way!

You have come this far in your preparation. You are beginning to take measurable steps toward realizing your vision. You are celebrating your successes and learning from your struggles. Every bit of it serves to prepare you for sustaining success once it is obtained. Oh, yes. Once you claim it, you have to keep it.

> **Once you claim it, you have to keep it.**

Just as a road trip requires adaptability and a willingness to embrace the unexpected, so does the pursuit of your dreams. You'll encounter detours, roadblocks, and scenic routes you never anticipated. But with each one, you'll grow more assertive, resilient, and determined to reach your ultimate destination.

So, buckle up, my friend. I believe your life is about to change. The one who put the desire inside of you will not give up on it, or you. Don't you quit, either. Look at this section of Paul's letter to the church in Rome, put so clearly in the *New Living Version*.

> "Now that we have been made right with God by putting our trust in Him, we have peace with Him. It is because of what our Lord Jesus Christ did for us. By putting our trust in God, He has given us His loving-favor and has received us. We are happy for the hope we have of sharing the shining-greatness of God. We are glad for our troubles also. We know that troubles help us learn not to give up. When we have learned not to give up, it shows we have stood the test. When we have stood the test, it gives us hope. Hope never makes us ashamed because the love of God has come into our hearts through the Holy Spirit Who was given to us.This verse speaks of God's swift and decisive action to fulfill His purposes in righteousness."
>
> — Romans 5:1-5 (NLV)

Say it with me:

> **It's my time. It's my season,**
>
> **It's God's will, and it's going to happen.**
>
> **My dream will come true.**

The Bible shows examples of ordinary people getting a dose of the unexpected — delays, disappointments, even death. What makes them heroes? Trust in God, knowing He has the final word on everything that touches us.

> **Joseph** faced betrayal by his brothers but rose to power in Egypt.
>
> **Moses** confronted Pharaoh's oppression, then led the Israelites to freedom
>
> **Job** endured immense suffering and loss but remained faithful to God and was ultimately restored.
>
> **David** battled enemies, including Goliath and King Saul, before becoming a victorious king through God's favor.
>
> **Esther** faced the threat of genocide and risked her life to save her people through courage and mediation with the king.
>
> **Daniel** was thrown into the lion's den for his faith, then he emerged unharmed due to God's protection.
>
> **Paul** was persecuted for his beliefs, but he continued to spread the Gospel and establish churches despite opposition.
>
> **Ruth** confronted challenges as a foreigner and widow, then found redemption through loyalty and faithfulness.
>
> **Abraham** endured trials and tests of faith before he became the father of many nations through God's promises.

Like many kids, the answer to "What do you want to be when you grow up" changed from moment to moment — and movie to movie. At one point, I was going to become an astronaut. One summer, I wanted to go to Space Camp. The inspiration for that career change from ballerina (or was it paleontologist?) was the movie *Space Camp* with Kate Capshaw. The young attendees of a space camp find themselves in space for real when their shuttle is accidentally launched into orbit. I was intrigued by space travel after seeing that movie, not to mention the good-looking bad boy played by Tate Donovan. I think about the terrified, unprepared teens depicted in the story.

These people who often disagreed were forced to get beyond their insecurities one minute and their pride the next to work together. They identified strengths and weaknesses, pooled their limited knowledge, and found solutions to return to where they were supposed to be — Earth.

Aside from being jettisoned into space, their journey sounds very familiar to what I've experienced. Does it to you? Life's events can make us feel like we've been launched into space, barely equipped to just keep from imploding. We face challenges and setbacks outside and within ourselves. Our dreams come true, sometimes a little differently than we'd envisioned. So, we adapt. We overcome.

The unexpected will happen. You can't prepare for what you don't see coming, but you know something will likely be down the road to test you. So, dig your heels in and refuse to let fear and uncertainty knock you off your feet. Gather whatever resources you can — knowledge, skills, mentors, truth, integrity, faith, and the full Armor of God (Ephesians 6:13-18). Be ready when and where you can, embrace the adventure, and dive headfirst into the unknown. You have the power to rise above adversity and seize the moment.

Begin by clearly defining your goals. What exactly do you want to achieve? Whether it's launching a business, embarking on a new career path, or mastering a new skill, be specific about your destination. Picture it as the mission's first step as you prepare to launch into the vast expanse of space.

By setting specific and measurable goals, you provide the coordinates that will guide your trajectory and propel you toward your dreams. So, take a moment to visualize where you want to go and define your goals with clarity and purpose, breaking each down into steps.

Creating smaller manageable tasks from your overarching goals will make the process less daunting and allow you to focus on one leg at a time. Create a timeline with deadlines for each task, just like a rocket has a checklist before liftoff. Organize your tasks and priorities using tools like to-do lists, calendars, or project management software. This will help you stay focused and track your progress along the way. Think of these tools as your spacecraft's control panels and navigation systems – they help you stay on course and make steady progress toward your destination.

Creating a to-do list is like laying out the blueprint for your mission. It breaks down your goals into manageable tasks, ensuring nothing gets overlooked or forgotten. Just as a rocket's engineers meticulously plan each stage of its journey, you'll carefully outline the steps you need to take to reach your goals.

Meanwhile, using a calendar helps you schedule your tasks and deadlines, ensuring you stay on track and meet your milestones. Think of it as setting the countdown timer for your launch – each day brings you one step closer to achieving your dreams.

And finally, project management software acts as your mission control center, providing a centralized hub for tracking your progress and collaborating with others. It allows you to monitor your tasks, allocate resources, and communicate with team members – just like mission control oversees every aspect of a spacecraft's mission from liftoff to landing.

By staying organized and using these tools effectively, you'll stay focused and maximize your productivity and efficiency. With each task completed, you'll feel the momentum building, like a rocket gathering speed as it climbs higher into the sky. Before you know it, you'll be ready to launch into the stratosphere of your dreams.

Just like a rocket needs the right fuel to reach its destination, you need to invest time in researching and gathering the resources necessary to achieve your goals. Picture your research and resources as the fuel and supplies needed to power your spacecraft on its mission. These resources are essential for success, whether it's books packed with knowledge, courses that provide valuable skills, mentors who offer guidance, or networking opportunities that connect you with like-minded individuals.

As you prepare for liftoff on the journey toward your dreams, focus on the critical step of developing a plan — just like a rocket needs a meticulously crafted flight plan to reach its destination. It is essential to identify potential obstacles along the way. Picture these obstacles as cosmic debris floating in your path – they have the potential to derail your journey if you're not prepared. Take the time to brainstorm strategies to overcome these obstacles, just as mission control plans for contingencies in a spacecraft's flight plan — but stay flexible.

Be prepared to adjust your plan as needed based on feedback and changing circumstances. Just as a rocket adjusts its trajectory mid-flight to navigate around unexpected obstacles, you may need to pivot and adapt your plan to stay on course toward your dreams.

As you develop your plan for liftoff, remember to think like an astronaut charting a course through the cosmos. Be thorough, be strategic, and be flexible. With a well-developed plan guiding your journey, you'll be well-equipped to navigate the challenges and opportunities ahead as you soar toward the stars of your dreams.

The most crucial step in turning your dreams into reality: taking action. Do something. Just like a rocket needs thrust to break free from Earth's gravity, you must take that first step to propel yourself toward your dreams.

Progress is progress, no matter how seemingly insignificant. Don't be discouraged by setbacks or challenges along the way – they're just part of the journey. Instead, stay focused on the next slight improvement you can make and keep moving forward, one task at a time. Keep pushing forward and building momentum; before you know it, you'll be well on your way to achieving your dreams. Don't give up!

Your dreams won't be realized overnight, just as Rome wasn't built in a day. But by staying persistent and maintaining a positive mindset, you'll keep moving forward, one step at a time.

As we approach the final countdown to liftoff, let's remember the importance of staying persistent and positive – just like the unwavering determination of an astronaut on a mission to the stars. Setbacks are like the gravitational pull trying to drag your rocket back to Earth. Instead of letting them hold you down, use them as opportunities to learn and grow. Just as a spacecraft adjusts and increases its thrusters to push through the Earth's atmosphere, use the excitement for your vision to propel you past the pull of exhaustion and frustration.

With persistence and positivity as your guiding stars, there's no limit to what you can achieve. So keep your eyes on the horizon, stay determined, and never lose sight of the dreams that await you among the stars. As you prepare for liftoff, remember that the journey may be challenging, but the rewards of reaching your dreams will make it all worthwhile.

By following these 7 strategies and staying committed to your vision, you'll be well on your way to turning your dreams into reality. Remember, the journey may be challenging at times, but the rewards of seeing your dreams come to fruition will make it all worthwhile. Keep believing in yourself and never stop daring to dream again. Your future awaits!

"Do or do not.
There is no try."

Yoda, *Star Wars: The Empire Strikes Back*

7 Game-Changing Habits for Transformational Outcomes

Implement Your Ideas

1. Define Your Goals.

Benefit: Clear goals give you a sense of direction and purpose, helping you focus on what's truly important to you.

2. Break It Down.

Benefit: By outlining specific, actionable steps, you create a roadmap that guides you towards your ultimate goal without getting overwhelmed.

3. Research and Inventory Resources.

Benefit: Helps in making informed decisions, optimizing resource use, planning strategically, and collaborating effectively.

4. Develop a Plan.

Benefit: Setting yourself up for success by defining what you want to achieve and outlining the steps to get there.

5. Stay Flexible.

Benefit: Striking a balance between having a clear plan and being open to change keep you moving forward, even when the unexpected happens.

6. Take Action.

Benefit: As you make progress, your confidence grows, reinforcing your commitment to your goals and your ability to reach them.

7. Stay Persistent and Positive.

Benefit: Positivity can lead to clearer thinking, better decision-making and improve relationships. Persistence will open up new possibilities.

DREAM COME TRUE

YOU

Throughout this book, you have read true stories of people who overcame adversity. Each story is a Dream Come True, like yours will one day be. Can you imagine it? Well, you had better. If you can't envision it, you won't be living it.

Someday, someone may include your journey to encourage others to **Dare to Dream Again**. What will that description look like?

In your final exercise with me, use these prompts to imagine and write your story about your future success as though it has already happened.

The Awards Ceremony: Envision yourself at an awards ceremony, receiving the highest honor in your field. What award are you receiving, and what accomplishments did you achieve to earn it?

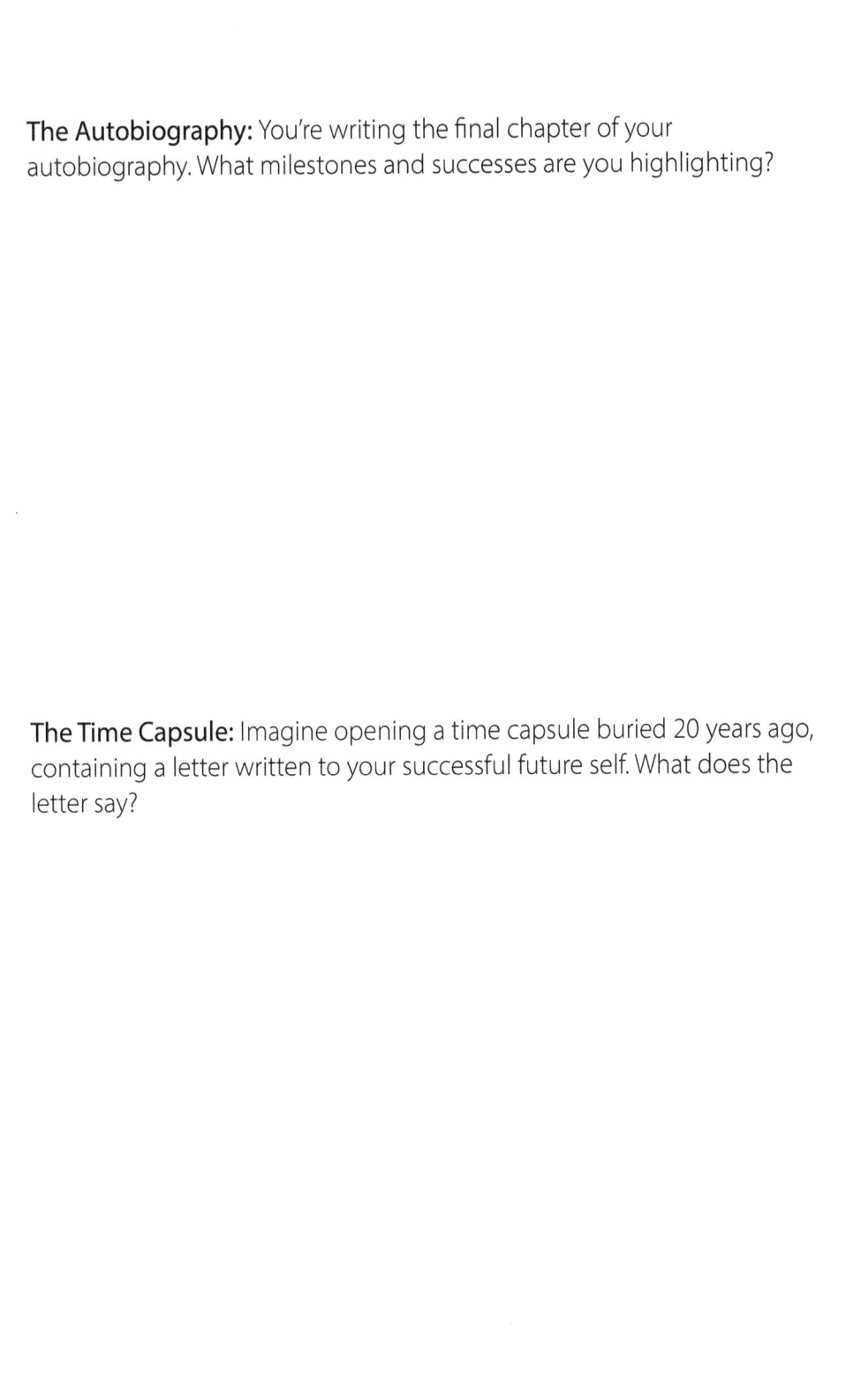

The Autobiography: You're writing the final chapter of your autobiography. What milestones and successes are you highlighting?

The Time Capsule: Imagine opening a time capsule buried 20 years ago, containing a letter written to your successful future self. What does the letter say?

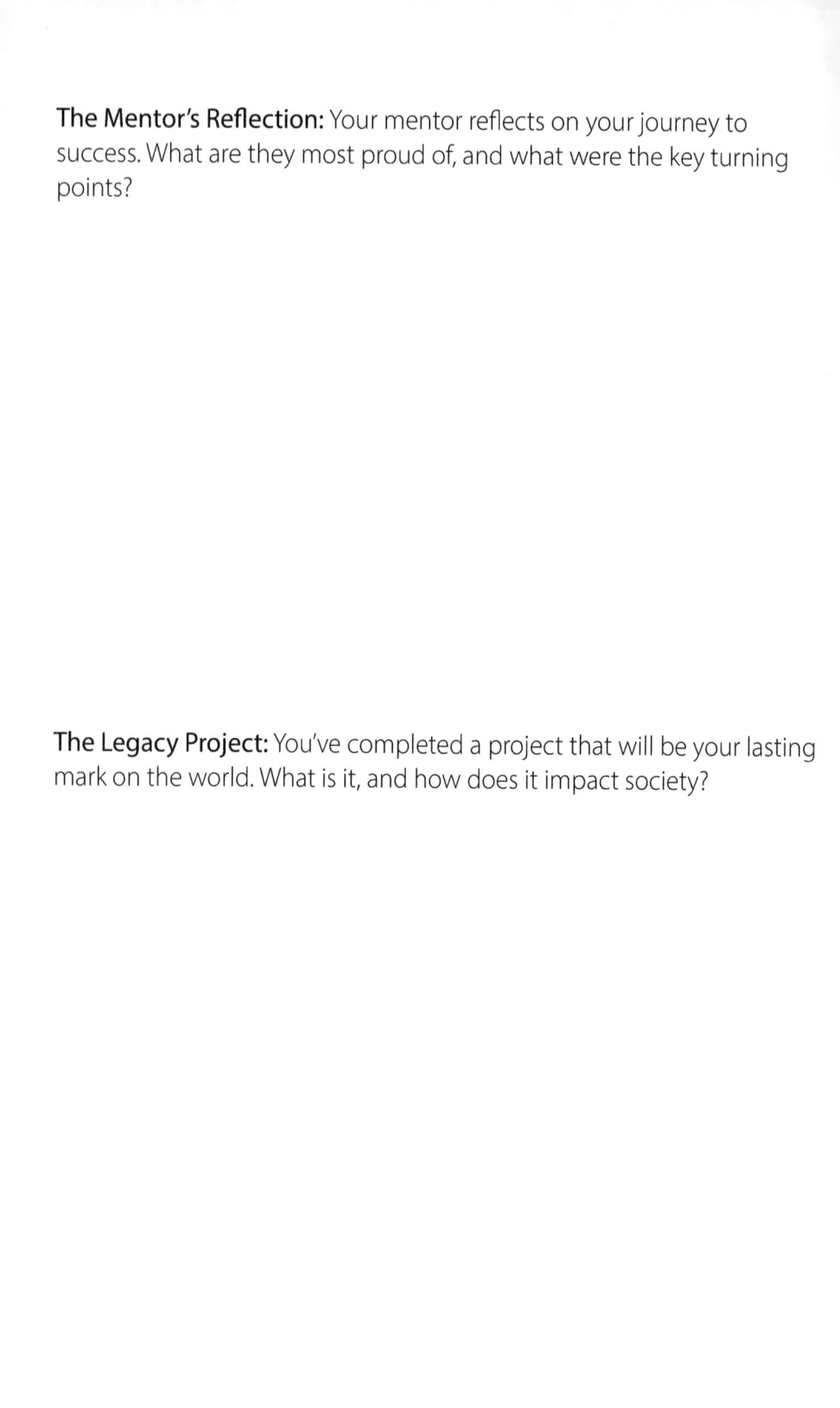

The Mentor's Reflection: Your mentor reflects on your journey to success. What are they most proud of, and what were the key turning points?

The Legacy Project: You've completed a project that will be your lasting mark on the world. What is it, and how does it impact society?

The Hall of Fame: You're being inducted into the Hall of Fame. What contributions and achievements have led to this moment?

> Every journey begins with a single step and a clear vision.
>
> Rosalinda Rivera

APPENDIX

PURPOSE WORKSHEET

PASSIONS AND PROFICIENCY

Complete the following to help identify your purpose and set goals.

1. My top three passions are _____

    _____

    _____

2. I am skilled in _____

    and have expertise in _____

3. In terms of industry, I am most interested in _____

    because _____

4. I believe there is a market opportunity or community need for a business/service that _____

    because _____

5. My available resources include (*financial, time, support network*) _____

    _____

6. My financial goal for the business is to *(e.g. generate a certain level of revenue and achieve profitability within a specific timeframe).*

_____

_____

7. I have received positive feedback on my business idea from *(e.g., friends, family, potential customers)*

_____

8. To test the viability of my business idea, I plan to *(e.g., conduct market research, create a prototype, launch a pilot program)*

_____

_____

9. In the next six months, I aim to achieve *(e.g., reach a certain number of customers, launch a product or service, secure funding)*

_____

_____

10. I am willing to adapt and refine my business idea based on *(e.g., feedback, market trends, changing circumstances)*

_____

_____

7 Game-Changing Habits for Transformational Outcomes

The Power of Vision

1. Clarity is Key.

   Benefit: Define your dreams with utmost clarity. The clearer your vision, the easier it is to manifest.

2. Visualize Daily.

   Benefit: Spend time each day vividly visualizing your goals as if they're already achieved.

3. Morning Rituals.

   Benefit: Start your day with empowering rituals that set the tone for success.

4. Action-Oriented Mindset.

Benefit: Approach each day with a relentless focus on taking massive action.

5. Master Your Emotions.

Benefit: Cultivate emotional mastery to stay resilient in the face of challenges.

6. Surround Yourself with Success.

Benefit: Surround yourself with high achievers who inspire and uplift you.

7. Never Settle.

Benefit: Refuse to settle for mediocrity. Strive for excellence in everything you do.and focus.

7 Game-Changing Habits for Transformational Outcomes

The Discipline of Execution

1. **Ruthless Prioritization.**

   Benefit: Identify your most important tasks and tackle them with laser focus.

2. **Daily Habits.**

   Benefit: Develop daily habits that align with your goals and propel you forward.

3. **Overcome Procrastination.**

   Benefit: Crush procrastination by breaking tasks into small, manageable steps.

4. Time Blocking.

Benefit: Schedule dedicated blocks of time for focused work on your most important goals.

5. Relentless Persistence.

Benefit: Embrace setbacks as stepping stones to success and never give up.

6. Continuous Learning.

Benefit: Commit to lifelong learning and growth to stay ahead in your field.

7. Celebrate Wins.

Benefit: Acknowledge and celebrate your progress, no matter how small.

7 Game-Changing Habits for Transformational Outcomes

The Mindset of Mastery

1. Unshakeable Belief.

    Benefit: Cultivate unshakeable belief in yourself and your ability to achieve anything.

2. Fearless Action.

    Benefit: Embrace fear and take bold, decisive action in spite of it.

3. Adaptability.

    Benefit: Stay flexible and adapt to changing circumstances with grace and resilience.

4. Fail Forward.

Benefit: Embrace failure as an inevitable part of the journey and a stepping stone to success.

5. Mindfulness Practice.

Benefit: Develop a daily mindfulness practice to stay present and focused.

6. Positive Affirmations.

Benefit: Flood your mind with positive affirmations that reinforce your worth and potential.

7. Gratitude Attitude.

Benefit: Cultivate an attitude of gratitude for everything you have and everything yet to come.

7 Game-Changing Habits for Transformational Outcomes

The Art of Influence

1. **Effective Communication.**

   Benefit: Hone your communication skills to inspire and influence others.

2. **Authentic Connection.**

   Benefit: Build genuine connections with people by showing empathy and understanding.

3. **Lead by Example.**

   Benefit: Lead by example and embody the qualities you wish to see in others.

4. Empower Others.

Benefit: Empower those around you to unlock their full potential and pursue their dreams.

5. Networking Mastery.

Benefit: Expand your network strategically and leverage relationships to create opportunities.

6. Relatability.

Benefit: Master the art of relatability and inspire others.

7. Legacy Building.

Benefit: Live each day with purpose and intention, leaving a lasting legacy of impact and inspiration.

ENDNOTES

1   Acharya, Riddhi. "Who Is Michael Phelps' Coach? Know Everything about the Legendary Swimmer's Mentor Who Currently Coaches in Arizona." *Sportskeeda*, Sportskeeda, 13 Feb. 2024, www.sportskeeda.com/swimming/who-michael-phelps-coach-know-everything-legendary-swimmer-s-mentor-currently-coaches-arizona.

2   Spielberg, Steven. 1985. *The Color Purple*. United States: Warner Bros

3   Person. "Oprah Winfrey's Official Biography." *Oprah.Com*, Oprah.com, 17 May 2011, www.oprah.com/pressroom/oprah-winfreys-official-biography/all.

4   Goalcast. "Top 20 Inspiring Oprah Winfrey Quotes That Will Empower You." *Goalcast*, 13 Jan. 2022, www.goalcast.com/top-20-inspiring-oprah-winfrey-quotes-that-will-empower-you/#:~:text=%E2%80%9CThe%20key%20to%20realizing%20a%20dream%20is%20to,the%20life%20of%20your%20dreams.%20%E2%80%95%20Oprah%20Winfrey.

5   Marie, Murielle. "3 Inspiring Women Who Achieved Their Big Dreams." *Murielle Marie*, murielle marie, 10 Feb. 2021, www.muriellemarie.com/blog/3-inspiring-women-who-achieved-their-big-dreams.

6   Warren, Rick. *The Purpose Driven Life: What on Earth Am I Here for*, Rick Warren. Zondervan, 2007.

7   Monteverde, Alejandro, director. *Cabrini. Angel Studios*, 2024

8   "Mother Cabrini." *Cabrini Mission Foundation*, cabrinifoundation.org/who-we-are/mother-cabrini/. Accessed 10 Apr. 2024.

9   "I've Fallen, and I Can't Get Up!" *Wikipedia*, Wikimedia Foundation, 7 Apr. 2024, en.wikipedia.org/wiki/I%27ve_fallen,_and_I_can%27t_get_up!

10   "The Flower Kings." *Wikipedia*, Wikimedia Foundation, 1 Apr. 2024, en.wikipedia.org/wiki/The_Flower_Kings.

11   Muccino, Gabriele. *The Pursuit of Happyness*. Columbia Pictures, 2006

12   Gee, Dawne. "One Step at a Time: The Story of Katherine Switzer." *Https://Www.Wave3.Com*, 28 Oct. 2017, www.wave3.com/story/36704241/one-step-at-a-time-the-story-of-katherine-switzer/.

13

ABOUT THE AUTHOR
Rosalinda Rivera

Rosalinda Rivera is a trailblazing entrepreneur who discovered her passion for business at a remarkably young age. Her journey began at the tender age of 7 when she fearlessly embarked on her first venture, cutting flowers from her mother's garden without permission and selling them to her neighbors. This initial taste of entrepreneurship ignited a fire within her, propelling her toward a future filled with innovation and success.

By the age of 11, Rosalinda's determination caught the attention of her neighbor, who generously provided her with boxes of jewelry and spare parts to jumpstart her own business. Undeterred by her young age, she harnessed her resourcefulness and began selling candy, cleverly packaging them in Ziplock bags tied around her bookbag. Her unwavering commitment to success pushed her to hustle tirelessly, whether to earn money for lunch or contribute towards making ends meet during her formative years.

While still in high school, at 16, Rosalinda took a significant leap by opening her first official storefront at the local super flea. Displaying her remarkable acumen, she would cross the street to the Goodwill store, purchasing toys and stuffed animals to resell at her burgeoning retail center. With a monthly rental cost of approximately $60, her efforts laid the foundation for her future achievements.

Rosalinda's true breakthrough came when financial constraints prevented her from pursuing a college education. However, her supportive parents connected her with a wholesaler from New York City. Harnessing her innate business savvy at age 17, she established "Eye For A Tie," specializing in silk ties, leather goods, and men's accessories. By the age of 19, Rosalinda secured her first lease in a prestigious national mall, cementing her status as a formidable force in the business world.

Over the course of three decades, Rosalinda Rivera's exemplary business skills have led her to collaborate with non-profit organizations and retail companies alike. She has honed her expertise in importing products from overseas, gaining a deep understanding of the intricacies involved in scaling a business from humble beginnings to overseeing, coaching, and training multi-million-dollar enterprises.

With an unwavering passion for helping others, Rosalinda finds immense joy in building brands, revitalizing struggling companies, and effectively conveying their unique messages. Her wealth of experience, combined with her astute marketing and branding insights, makes her a trusted partner for businesses seeking transformative growth.

She hosts "Faith Fuel" on the Charisma Podcast Network, and Rosalinda is an internationally known speaker and author. Rosalinda also served as Associate Producer on Victor, a movie about her father's journey from drugs and gangs to Jesus and redemption.

Rosalinda has been reaching out to families in crisis, poverty, and hopelessness for more than twenty-five years to bring them healing and a positive future. With power and passion, she connects to the hearts of people everywhere as she emanates the grace and wisdom harvested throughout her years of public service.

Known as a Change Strategist, Rosalinda regularly speaks at leadership conferences, churches, corporations, and seminars. She also hosts the powerful Bella Women's Conference each year, touching thousands of women's lives.

Rosalinda has been a featured presenter and ministered across the U.S. and throughout the world. From the White House to the local community, Rosalinda is nationally recognized for her impact in bringing hope to the hopeless. Rosalinda was appointed to the Board of Governors of the National Association of Nonprofit Organizations & Executives, headquartered in Washington, DC.

Rosalinda Rivera, a humorous and fun-loving individual, finds joy in life. Along with her husband, Carlos Rivera, they serve as Senior Pastors of *New Life Outreach Intl.* in Richmond, Virginia. She is the President of *New Life Clinical Services of Virginia, New Life Enterprises, Wash N Roll Car Wash, New Life Thrift Store, Lionlab Publishing*, and *Lionlab Promos*. No business opportunity is more important than her husband, children, and family: Alana, Son-in-Love Joey Martinez, new grandbaby Joshua; Gabriel and Daughter-in-Love Breanna Rivera; and Victor Rivera. Rosalinda takes pride in being a loving mother to three children, and they share their home with a delightful dog named Armani.

Her favorite hobby is vacationing with her family, creating Cherished memories together. She has been happily married to her beloved spouse, Carlos, and they continue to enjoy activities like salsa dancing, dining out, and going to the movies.

MORE FROM ROSALINDA RIVERA

MORE in the **DARE** Series

SHE is a **HERO**

GARNER SUCCESS in Business and Life

FROM CARLOS RIVERA

Walk Right.
Walk in Power.
Walk in the Spirit.

YOU'RE MORE THAN WELCOME.
YOU ARE <u>WANTED</u>!

New Life Outreach is a family — a place you can call home. It's where you can find hope, healing, and purpose. Over the years, this family has grown and changed, but one thing will always stay the same: Our love for Jesus and for each other. No matter where you're at in your journey, you can be confident that you're more than welcome at New Life — you're wanted.

Pastors Carlos & Rosalinda Rivera
Lead Pastors

FIND OUT MORE ABOUT NEW LIFE!

NEW LIFE
OUTREACH CHURCH

Sunday Worship — Sunday 9:00 AM

Sunday Worship — Sunday 11:00 AM

Sunday Spanish Service — Sunday 2:30 PM

Wednesday Worship Service — Wednesday 7:00 PM

WELCOME HOME!

1005 Turner Road
N. Chesterfield, VA 23225

804-276-6767

newlifeoutreach.church

The New Life App is LIVE!!!!

Your place for:
- Messages
- Connecting
- Giving
- Growing

Download it today!

App Store • Google Play

Text keyword **NLO app** to **77977**